I0454329

Your Sixth Move

Mastering Strategic Execution

OnePurp's Team

To all those who dare to dream, plan, and execute,
This book is dedicated to you.

May your strategic journeys be filled with wisdom and
success.

CONTENTS

INTRODUCTION

In the world of business strategy, the journey from crafting a brilliant plan to its successful execution is often fraught with challenges. Many companies excel at brainstorming innovative strategies, but falter when it comes to translating these ideas into concrete actions that yield results. It's in this critical space, the gap between strategy and implementation, that we introduce the concept of "Your Sixth Move."

While the concept of the sixth move is not explicitly outlined in Patrick Bet-David's "Your Next Five Moves," it's a theoretical underpinning that this book takes to the next level. We consider it as the essential missing piece that's inherent in the strategies laid out in the predecessor. In essence, it's the glue that binds your first five moves into a cohesive, results-driven action plan.

Imagine a world where the gap between a brilliant strategic plan and its actual implementation has been effectively bridged. This is where "Your Sixth Move" comes into play. We explore the intricate art of strategic execution in its entirety. It's not just about having a great plan; it's about making that plan work in the real world.

The critical components of this book include a comprehensive look at the role of project management in executing strategies. We dive into the nitty-gritty of project planning, tracking, and management, providing you with tips, techniques, and best practices for ensuring your projects align perfectly with your overarching strategy.

Resource allocation is another key facet of executing strategies. Whether it's finances, personnel, or technology, we explore the strategies that can help you optimize resource utilization, ensuring that your execution stays on course.

In a fast-paced world, maintaining agility in execution is essential. We highlight the need for adaptability and provide insights into methods for staying flexible and responsive to changes. The case studies of strategic execution featured in this book shed light on the real-world applications of these strategies, extracting valuable lessons from businesses that have mastered execution.

Overcoming common execution challenges is a critical aspect of this book. We address resistance to change and the unpredictability of disruptive events, offering practical solutions and strategies to navigate these obstacles effectively.

The role of leadership in execution is another core element. We explore the qualities and behaviors of effective leaders in the execution process and discuss how leaders can inspire teams and drive successful execution.

Measuring success and continuous improvement are key to maintaining forward momentum. We explain the importance of metrics and Key Performance Indicators (KPIs) in assessing execution and emphasize the value of learning from execution experiences and continuously improving your approach.

As you progress through the book, you'll embark on a journey to create your own personal execution plan. This plan is more than a document; it's a roadmap to transform your strategy into reality.

"Your Sixth Move: Mastering Strategic Execution" is not just a theoretical concept; it's the culmination of a comprehensive guide that empowers you to bridge the gap between strategic planning and its successful implementation. This book equips you with the knowledge, strategies, and tools to become a master of the art of strategic execution, turning your visionary ideas into tangible achievements.

1. THE ART OF STRATEGY RECAP

1.1 UNDERSTANDING THE FUNDAMENTALS OF STRATEGY

In order to master strategic execution, it is crucial to have a solid understanding of the fundamentals of strategy. Strategy is the art of planning and directing actions to achieve specific goals or objectives. It involves making choices about where to compete, how to compete, and how to allocate resources effectively.

The Importance of Strategy

Strategy provides a roadmap for success. It helps organizations navigate through uncertainty and complexity by providing a clear direction and purpose. Without a well-defined strategy, organizations may find themselves drifting aimlessly, lacking focus, and struggling to achieve their desired outcomes.

The Elements of Strategy

A successful strategy consists of several key elements:

Vision and Mission: A clear vision and mission statement provide a sense of purpose and direction. The vision describes the desired future state, while the mission outlines the organization's core purpose and reason for existence.

Goals and Objectives: Goals and objectives are the specific outcomes that an organization aims to achieve. They should be measurable, time-bound, and aligned with the overall strategy.

Competitive Advantage: Competitive advantage refers to the unique strengths and capabilities that set an organization apart from its competitors. It can be achieved through factors such as cost leadership, differentiation, or focus on a specific niche.

Market Analysis: Understanding the market and industry dynamics is essential for developing an effective strategy. This involves analyzing customer needs, competitor behavior, and market trends to identify opportunities and threats.

Strategic Options: Strategy is about making choices. Organizations must evaluate different strategic options and select the ones that align with their goals and resources. This may involve deciding on the target market, product positioning, pricing strategy, and distribution channels.

Strategic Frameworks

To help make sense of the complex strategic landscape, various frameworks and models have been developed. These frameworks provide a structured approach to analyzing and formulating strategy. Some commonly used frameworks include:

SWOT Analysis: SWOT stands for Strengths, Weaknesses, Opportunities, and Threats. This framework helps organizations assess their internal strengths and weaknesses, as well as external opportunities and threats, to identify strategic priorities.

Porter's Five Forces: Developed by Michael Porter, this framework analyzes the competitive forces within an industry, including the threat of new entrants, bargaining power of suppliers and buyers, threat of substitutes, and intensity of competitive rivalry. It helps organizations understand the attractiveness of an industry and develop strategies to gain a competitive advantage.

Value Chain Analysis: The value chain is a series of activities that organizations perform to deliver a product or service to customers. This framework helps identify the primary and support activities that create value and can be optimized to achieve a competitive advantage.

Ansoff Matrix: The Ansoff Matrix helps organizations identify growth strategies by considering the market and product dimensions. It provides a framework for evaluating options such as market penetration, market development, product development, and diversification.

Aligning Strategy with Execution

While strategy provides the direction, execution is the process of implementing the strategy effectively. It involves translating the strategic plan into action, allocating resources, and monitoring progress. Strategy and execution are interdependent and must be aligned for success. A well-crafted strategy without effective execution is unlikely to achieve the desired outcomes.

In the following sections of this book, we will explore the key concepts and frameworks that underpin strategic execution. We will delve into analyzing competitive advantage, developing strategic objectives, and creating an execution plan. By understanding these fundamentals, you will be better equipped to navigate the complexities of strategic execution and achieve your desired goals.

1.2 KEY CONCEPTS AND FRAMEWORKS

In order to master strategic execution, it is essential to understand the key concepts and frameworks that underpin effective implementation. This section will provide an overview of some of the most important concepts and frameworks that can guide your execution efforts.

1.2.1 Strategy Execution Framework

One of the fundamental frameworks for strategic execution is the Strategy Execution Framework. This framework provides a structured approach to translating strategic goals into actionable plans and executing them effectively. It consists of four key components:

Strategy Development: This involves the process of formulating a clear and compelling strategy that aligns with the organization's vision and goals. It includes conducting a thorough analysis of the internal and external environment, identifying strategic objectives, and developing a roadmap for execution.

Strategy Communication: Once the strategy is developed, it is crucial to effectively communicate it to all stakeholders within the organization. This ensures that everyone understands the strategic direction and their role in executing it. Clear and consistent communication helps to align efforts and foster a shared understanding of the strategy.

Strategy Alignment: Strategy alignment involves aligning all aspects of the organization, including people, processes, and resources, with the strategic objectives. This requires ensuring that the right people are in the right roles, establishing clear performance metrics, and aligning incentives and rewards with the strategic goals. It also involves creating a culture that supports and reinforces the execution of the strategy.

Strategy Execution: The final component of the Strategy Execution Framework is the actual execution of the strategy. This involves implementing the action plans, monitoring progress, and making necessary adjustments along the way. It requires effective project management, resource allocation, and continuous improvement practices to ensure that the strategy is executed successfully.

By following this framework, organizations can enhance their ability to execute their strategies effectively and achieve their desired outcomes.

1.2.2 Balanced Scorecard
The Balanced Scorecard is another widely used framework that helps organizations translate

their strategic objectives into a set of performance measures. It provides a balanced view of performance by considering four key perspectives:

Financial Perspective: This perspective focuses on financial measures such as revenue growth, profitability, and return on investment. It helps organizations assess the financial impact of their strategic initiatives and ensure that they are contributing to the overall financial health of the organization.

Customer Perspective: The customer perspective looks at measures related to customer satisfaction, loyalty, and market share. It helps organizations understand how well they are meeting customer needs and whether their strategic initiatives are driving customer value.

Internal Process Perspective: This perspective examines the internal processes and activities that are critical to delivering value to customers. It includes measures related to operational efficiency, quality, and innovation. By monitoring these measures, organizations can identify areas for improvement and ensure that their processes are aligned with their strategic objectives.

Learning and Growth Perspective: The learning and growth perspective focuses on the organization's ability to learn, innovate, and develop its people and capabilities. It includes measures related to employee satisfaction, skills development, and organizational culture. By investing in learning and growth, organizations can build the capabilities needed to execute their strategies effectively.

The Balanced Scorecard provides a comprehensive framework for measuring and managing performance in a balanced and holistic manner. It helps organizations track progress towards their strategic objectives and make informed decisions to drive execution.

1.2.3 SWOT Analysis

SWOT analysis is a widely used tool for assessing an organization's internal strengths and weaknesses, as well as external opportunities and threats. It provides a structured approach to understanding the strategic context and identifying key factors that can impact execution.

Strengths: These are the internal capabilities and resources that give the organization a competitive advantage. By leveraging strengths, organizations can capitalize on opportunities and overcome challenges during execution.

Weaknesses: Weaknesses are internal factors that hinder the organization's ability to execute its strategy effectively. Identifying weaknesses is crucial for developing mitigation strategies and allocating resources appropriately.

Opportunities: Opportunities are external factors

that can be leveraged to achieve strategic objectives. By identifying and capitalizing on opportunities, organizations can enhance their chances of successful execution.

Threats: Threats are external factors that can pose risks to the organization's strategy execution. By understanding and mitigating threats, organizations can minimize potential disruptions and ensure smoother execution.

SWOT analysis provides a comprehensive view of the internal and external factors that can impact execution. It helps organizations identify areas of focus and develop strategies to maximize their chances of success.

1.2.4 Change Management Models

Change management is an integral part of strategic execution, as it involves navigating the challenges and resistance that often accompany organizational change. Several change management models can guide organizations through the process of implementing strategic initiatives:

Kotter's 8-Step Change Model: Developed by John Kotter, this model provides a step-by-step approach to managing change. It emphasizes the importance of creating a sense of urgency, building a guiding coalition, and communicating the vision for change effectively.

Lewin's Change Management Model: Lewin's model suggests that change occurs in three stages: unfreezing, changing, and refreezing. It emphasizes the need to create a supportive environment for change, involve key stakeholders, and reinforce new behaviors to ensure lasting change.

ADKAR Model: The ADKAR model focuses on individual change by addressing five key elements: awareness, desire, knowledge, ability, and reinforcement. It provides a framework for understanding and managing the psychological and behavioral aspects of change.

By applying these change management models, organizations can navigate the complexities of change and increase the likelihood of successful execution.

Understanding these key concepts and frameworks is essential for mastering strategic execution. They provide a solid foundation for developing effective execution plans, aligning resources, and managing change. In the following sections, we will explore these concepts in more detail and provide practical guidance on how to apply them in your execution efforts.

1.3 ANALYZING COMPETITIVE ADVANTAGE

In the world of business, competition is inevitable.

Every company, regardless of its size or industry, must face the challenge of competing against others to gain a larger market share and achieve sustainable growth. To succeed in this competitive landscape, it is crucial for organizations to understand and analyze their competitive advantage.

Understanding Competitive Advantage

Competitive advantage refers to the unique strengths and capabilities that set a company apart from its competitors. It is what gives a company an edge in the market and allows it to outperform its rivals. Analyzing competitive advantage involves identifying and evaluating these strengths and understanding how they contribute to the company's success.

There are two main types of competitive advantage: cost advantage and differentiation advantage. A cost advantage is achieved when a company can produce goods or services at a lower cost than its competitors. This allows the company to offer lower prices to customers while still maintaining profitability. On the other hand, a differentiation advantage is achieved when a company offers unique and superior products or services that are valued by customers. This allows the company to command higher prices and build customer loyalty.

Analyzing Competitive Advantage

To analyze competitive advantage, companies need to conduct a thorough assessment of their internal and external environments. This involves evaluating various factors that contribute to their competitive position, such as:

Market Analysis: Companies need to understand the dynamics of the market in which they operate. This includes analyzing the size of the market, its growth potential, and the behavior of customers and competitors. By understanding the market, companies can identify opportunities and threats that may impact their competitive advantage.

Internal Analysis: Companies must assess their internal strengths and weaknesses. This involves evaluating their resources, capabilities, and core competencies. Resources can include physical assets, intellectual property, and human capital, while capabilities refer to the company's ability to perform specific activities. By identifying their strengths and weaknesses, companies can leverage their advantages and address any areas of improvement.

Competitor Analysis: Understanding the competition is essential for analyzing competitive advantage. Companies need to identify their direct and indirect competitors and evaluate their strategies, strengths, and weaknesses. This analysis helps companies identify areas where they can differentiate themselves and gain a competitive edge.

Customer Analysis: Companies must understand their target customers and their needs, preferences, and buying behavior. By analyzing customer segments, companies can tailor their products or services to meet specific customer demands and create a unique value proposition.

SWOT Analysis: A SWOT analysis is a useful tool for analyzing competitive advantage. It involves evaluating the company's strengths, weaknesses, opportunities, and threats. By identifying these factors, companies can develop strategies to capitalize on their strengths, address weaknesses, exploit opportunities, and mitigate threats.

Leveraging Competitive Advantage

Once a company has analyzed its competitive advantage, it can leverage it to drive strategic execution and achieve its goals. Here are some ways companies can leverage their competitive advantage:

Differentiation Strategy: Companies with a differentiation advantage can focus on creating unique and superior products or services that meet customer needs better than their competitors. By continuously innovating and delivering exceptional value, these companies can attract and retain customers.

Cost Leadership Strategy: Companies with a cost advantage can focus on reducing costs and offering competitive prices to customers. By optimizing their operations, streamlining processes, and leveraging economies of scale, these companies can achieve higher profitability and gain market share.

Focus Strategy: Companies can also leverage their competitive advantage by focusing on a specific market segment or niche. By tailoring their products or services to meet the unique needs of a particular customer group, these companies can establish a strong position in that market and build customer loyalty.

Collaboration and Partnerships: Companies can leverage their competitive advantage by forming strategic alliances, partnerships, or collaborations with other organizations. By combining their strengths and resources, companies can create synergies and gain a competitive edge in the market.

Continuous Improvement: Competitive advantage is not static; it requires continuous improvement and adaptation. Companies must constantly monitor the market, analyze competitors, and identify emerging trends and opportunities. By staying agile and responsive, companies can maintain their competitive advantage and stay ahead of the competition.

In conclusion, analyzing competitive advantage is a critical step in strategic execution. By understanding their unique strengths and capabilities, companies can develop strategies that leverage their competitive advantage and drive success in the marketplace. Through market analysis, internal analysis, competitor analysis, and customer analysis, companies can gain valuable insights that inform their strategic decisions. By leveraging their competitive advantage effectively, companies can differentiate themselves, achieve cost leadership, or focus on specific market segments, ultimately leading to sustainable growth and success.

1.4 DEVELOPING STRATEGIC OBJECTIVES
In order to effectively execute a strategic plan, it is crucial to develop clear and actionable strategic objectives. Strategic objectives serve as the guiding principles that drive the execution process and help organizations achieve their desired outcomes. In this section, we will explore the importance of developing strategic objectives and provide practical guidance on how to create them.

The Role of Strategic Objectives
Strategic objectives provide a clear direction and purpose for the execution of a strategic plan. They serve as the foundation upon which all other execution activities are built. By defining specific and measurable objectives, organizations can

align their resources, efforts, and initiatives towards a common goal.

Strategic objectives also help organizations prioritize their actions and make informed decisions. They provide a framework for evaluating potential opportunities and determining which ones are most aligned with the overall strategy. By focusing on the objectives that are most critical to success, organizations can allocate their resources effectively and avoid spreading themselves too thin.

Characteristics of Effective Strategic Objectives

Effective strategic objectives possess certain characteristics that make them actionable and measurable. Here are some key characteristics to consider when developing strategic objectives:

Specific: Strategic objectives should be clear and specific, leaving no room for ambiguity. They should clearly define what needs to be achieved and provide a clear target for the execution team to work towards.

Measurable: Objectives should be measurable so that progress can be tracked and evaluated. This allows organizations to determine whether they are on track to achieve their objectives or if adjustments need to be made.

Aligned: Strategic objectives should be aligned with the overall strategic direction of the organization. They should support the overarching goals and vision, ensuring that all efforts are moving in the same direction.

Time-bound: Objectives should have a defined timeline or deadline for completion. This helps create a sense of urgency and ensures that progress is being made within a reasonable time frame.

Challenging yet attainable: Strategic objectives should be ambitious enough to drive growth and progress but also realistic and attainable. Setting objectives that are too easy may not inspire the necessary effort, while setting objectives that are too difficult may lead to frustration and demotivation.

Developing Strategic Objectives

Developing strategic objectives requires a systematic approach that involves input from key stakeholders and a thorough understanding of the organization's strategic priorities. Here are some steps to guide you through the process:

Review the strategic plan: Start by reviewing the organization's strategic plan and identifying the key goals and priorities. This will provide the context for developing strategic objectives that are aligned with the overall strategy.

Engage stakeholders: Involve key stakeholders,

such as senior leaders, department heads, and frontline employees, in the objective-setting process. Their input and perspectives can provide valuable insights and ensure buy-in from all levels of the organization.

Brainstorm objectives: Conduct brainstorming sessions to generate a list of potential strategic objectives. Encourage creativity and open discussion to explore different possibilities and perspectives.

Evaluate and prioritize: Evaluate each potential objective based on its alignment with the strategic plan, feasibility, and potential impact. Prioritize the objectives that are most critical to the organization's success and have the highest potential for achieving the desired outcomes.

Refine and finalize: Refine the selected objectives by making them more specific, measurable, and time-bound. Ensure that they are aligned with the overall strategy and reflect the organization's priorities. Seek feedback from stakeholders to ensure their understanding and agreement.

Communicate and cascade: Once the strategic objectives are finalized, communicate them to all relevant stakeholders. Cascade the objectives down to different levels of the organization, ensuring that everyone understands their role in achieving the objectives.

Monitor and adjust: Continuously monitor the progress towards the strategic objectives and make adjustments as needed. Regularly review and evaluate the objectives to ensure they remain relevant and aligned with the evolving needs of the organization.

By following these steps, organizations can develop strategic objectives that provide a clear roadmap for execution and increase the likelihood of achieving their desired outcomes.

Developing strategic objectives is a critical step in the execution process. Strategic objectives provide the direction, focus, and purpose needed to drive successful execution. By ensuring that objectives are specific, measurable, aligned, time-bound, and challenging yet attainable, organizations can set themselves up for success. Through a systematic approach that involves stakeholder engagement, brainstorming, evaluation, refinement, and communication, organizations can develop strategic objectives that guide their execution efforts and lead to the achievement of their strategic goals.

2. THE MISSING PIECE – <u>EXECUTION</u>

2.1 THE IMPORTANCE OF EXECUTION

Execution is the missing piece that transforms strategy from mere ideas into tangible results. It is the process of translating strategic plans into action, ensuring that every step is taken to achieve the desired outcomes. While strategy sets the direction and defines the goals, execution is what brings those goals to life.

Without effective execution, even the most brilliant strategies will remain nothing more than theoretical concepts. Execution is what separates successful organizations from those that struggle to achieve their objectives. It is the driving force behind progress and the catalyst for growth.

The importance of execution cannot be overstated. It is the difference between a vision that remains unrealized and a vision that becomes a reality. Without execution, strategies are merely wishful thinking, and organizations are left stagnant, unable to adapt to changing market conditions or capitalize on emerging opportunities.

One of the key reasons why execution is so crucial is that it bridges the gap between planning and results. Many organizations invest significant time and resources in developing strategic plans, but they often fall short when it comes to executing those plans effectively. This execution gap can be attributed to various factors, including poor communication, lack of accountability, and inadequate resource allocation.

Execution is not just about following a set of predefined steps; it requires a proactive and dynamic approach. It involves making informed decisions, adapting to changing circumstances, and overcoming obstacles along the way. Successful execution requires a combination of strategic thinking, operational excellence, and effective leadership.

Furthermore, execution is essential for building credibility and trust. When organizations consistently deliver on their promises and achieve their strategic objectives, they earn the confidence of their stakeholders. This includes customers, employees, investors, and partners. By demonstrating their ability to execute, organizations can attract and retain top talent, secure funding, and build strong relationships with their customers and partners.

Another critical aspect of execution is its impact on organizational culture. When execution is prioritized and embedded within the DNA of an organization, it creates a culture of accountability, discipline, and continuous improvement. Employees become more engaged and motivated, knowing that their efforts are directly contributing to the organization's success. This culture of execution fosters innovation, collaboration, and a sense of ownership among team members.

In today's fast-paced and competitive business environment, execution is more important than ever. Organizations that can execute their strategies effectively gain a significant competitive advantage. They can respond quickly to market changes, seize opportunities, and outperform their competitors. In contrast, organizations that struggle with execution find themselves falling behind, unable to keep up with the demands of the market.

To excel in execution, organizations must develop a systematic approach that aligns their resources, processes, and people with their strategic objectives. This requires clear communication, effective project management, efficient resource allocation, and a culture that embraces agility and continuous improvement.

In the following sections of this book, we will explore the common challenges organizations face in execution, the role of strategy in execution, and the blueprint for strategic execution. We will delve into the principles of effective project management, resource allocation, and maintaining agility in execution. We will also examine real-world case studies, identify common execution challenges, and discuss the role of leadership in driving successful execution.

By mastering the art of execution, you will be able to turn your strategic plans into reality, achieve your goals, and propel your organization towards success. It is time to bridge the gap between strategy and execution and unlock the full potential of your organization.

2.2 COMMON EXECUTION CHALLENGES

Executing a strategic plan is not without its challenges. In fact, many organizations struggle to effectively implement their strategies due to a variety of common execution challenges. Understanding these challenges is crucial for mastering strategic execution. In this section, we will explore some of the most prevalent obstacles that organizations face when it comes to executing their strategies.

Lack of Clarity and Alignment

One of the primary challenges in executing a strategy is the lack of clarity and alignment within the organization. Without a clear understanding of the strategic objectives and how they align with the overall vision, employees may struggle to prioritize their efforts and make informed decisions. This lack of alignment can lead to confusion, inefficiency, and ultimately, the failure to achieve desired outcomes.

To overcome this challenge, it is essential to communicate the strategy effectively throughout the organization. This involves clearly articulating the strategic objectives, explaining how they align with the overall vision, and ensuring that every employee understands their role in executing the strategy. Regular communication and feedback loops can help maintain alignment and ensure that everyone is working towards the same goals.

Insufficient Resources and Capacity

Another common challenge in executing a strategy is the lack of sufficient resources and capacity. Organizations often underestimate the resources required to implement their strategic initiatives, leading to delays, budget overruns, and compromised quality. Insufficient capacity, whether it be in terms of manpower, technology, or infrastructure, can hinder the execution process and prevent the organization from achieving its strategic objectives.

To address this challenge, it is crucial to conduct a thorough resource assessment during the planning phase. This assessment should identify the resources needed to execute the strategy and determine whether the organization has the necessary capacity to meet those requirements. If there are resource gaps, proactive measures should be taken to secure the necessary resources, whether through hiring, training, or outsourcing.

Resistance to Change

Resistance to change is a significant challenge that organizations often face during the execution of their strategies. Employees may resist new processes, technologies, or organizational structures, fearing the unknown or feeling threatened by the changes. This resistance can impede progress, create a negative work environment, and ultimately derail the execution of the strategy.

To overcome resistance to change, it is essential to involve employees in the strategic planning process from the beginning. By engaging them in the decision-making and providing opportunities for input, employees are more likely to embrace the changes and feel a sense of ownership in the execution process. Additionally, effective change management strategies, such as clear communication, training, and support, can help alleviate resistance and facilitate a smoother transition.

Lack of Accountability

A lack of accountability is another common challenge that can hinder strategic execution. When individuals and teams are not held accountable for their actions and outcomes, it becomes difficult to track progress, identify bottlenecks, and make necessary adjustments. Without accountability, the execution process can become fragmented, with no clear ownership or responsibility for achieving results.

To address this challenge, it is crucial to establish a culture of accountability within the organization. This involves setting clear expectations, defining roles and responsibilities, and implementing mechanisms for tracking and evaluating progress. Regular performance reviews, feedback sessions, and recognition of achievements can also help foster a sense of accountability and motivate individuals and teams to deliver on their commitments.

Lack of Flexibility and Adaptability

In today's rapidly changing business environment, organizations must be flexible and adaptable in their execution approach. However, many organizations struggle with this challenge, as they are often bound by rigid processes, hierarchies, and bureaucratic structures. This lack of flexibility can hinder the organization's ability to respond to unexpected challenges, seize new opportunities, and adjust the execution plan as needed.

To overcome this challenge, organizations should embrace a more agile approach to execution. This involves empowering employees to make decisions, encouraging experimentation and learning from failures, and fostering a culture that values adaptability and continuous improvement. By embracing flexibility and adaptability, organizations can navigate uncertainties and changes more effectively, increasing their chances of successful strategy execution.

In conclusion, executing a strategic plan is not without its challenges. Lack of clarity and alignment, insufficient resources and capacity, resistance to change, lack of accountability, and lack of flexibility and adaptability are some of the common obstacles organizations face when it comes to executing their strategies. By understanding and addressing these challenges, organizations can enhance their ability to master strategic execution and achieve their desired outcomes.

2.3 THE EXECUTION GAP

In the previous section, we discussed the common challenges that organizations face when it comes to executing their strategies. Now, let's delve deeper into one of the most significant obstacles: the execution gap.

Understanding the Execution Gap

The execution gap refers to the disparity between a company's strategic intentions and its ability to effectively implement those strategies. It is the space where many well-crafted plans fail to materialize into tangible results. This gap can occur due to various reasons, including poor communication, lack of alignment, inadequate resources, and resistance to change.

The execution gap is a critical issue that organizations must address if they want to achieve their strategic objectives. Without bridging this gap, even the most brilliant strategies will remain mere ideas on paper, failing to create the desired impact.

Causes of the Execution Gap

Several factors contribute to the existence of the execution gap. Let's explore some of the most common causes:

Lack of Clarity and Alignment

One of the primary reasons for the execution gap is a lack of clarity and alignment within the organization. When strategic objectives are not clearly defined or communicated, it becomes challenging for employees to understand their roles and responsibilities. This lack of clarity can lead to confusion, inefficiency, and ultimately, a failure to execute the strategy effectively.

Insufficient Resources and Support

Another significant cause of the execution gap is the lack of adequate resources and support. Without the necessary tools, technology, and manpower, executing a strategy becomes an uphill battle. Insufficient resources can hinder progress, delay timelines, and compromise the overall success of the execution.

Resistance to Change

Resistance to change is a common barrier that organizations face during the execution of their strategies. Employees may resist new initiatives due to fear, uncertainty, or a lack of understanding about the benefits of the proposed changes. This resistance can slow down the execution process and create roadblocks that need to be overcome.

Ineffective Communication

Effective communication is crucial for successful execution. When communication channels break down or become ineffective, it can lead to misunderstandings, misalignment, and a lack of coordination. Poor communication can result in missed deadlines, duplicated efforts, and a failure to achieve the desired outcomes.

Inadequate Performance Measurement

Without proper performance measurement systems in place, it becomes challenging to track progress and identify areas for improvement. Organizations need to establish key performance indicators (KPIs) and regularly monitor and evaluate their execution efforts. Without this feedback loop, it is difficult to make informed decisions and adjust strategies as needed.

Closing the Execution Gap

Closing the execution gap requires a proactive and systematic approach. Here are some strategies to help organizations bridge the gap and improve their execution capabilities:

Clear and Aligned Objectives
Start by ensuring that your strategic objectives are clear, specific, and aligned with the overall vision of the organization. Communicate these objectives effectively to all stakeholders, ensuring that everyone understands their role in executing the strategy.

Resource Allocation
Allocate the necessary resources, including financial, human, and technological, to support the execution of your strategy. Conduct a thorough assessment of your resource needs and make strategic investments to fill any gaps.

Effective Communication
Establish open and transparent communication channels throughout the organization. Encourage feedback, provide regular updates, and foster a culture of collaboration. Effective communication will help align everyone towards the common goal and minimize misunderstandings.

Change Management
Implement a robust change management process to address resistance and facilitate a smooth transition. Involve employees in the decision-making process, provide training and support, and clearly communicate the benefits of the proposed changes.

Performance Measurement and Evaluation

Develop a comprehensive performance measurement system that tracks progress, identifies bottlenecks, and provides insights for improvement. Regularly evaluate your execution efforts against established KPIs and make data-driven decisions to optimize your strategies.

The execution gap is a significant challenge that organizations face when trying to implement their strategies successfully. By understanding the causes of this gap and implementing strategies to bridge it, organizations can improve their execution capabilities and achieve their strategic objectives. In the next section, we will explore the role of strategy in execution and how the two are interconnected.

2.4 THE ROLE OF STRATEGY IN EXECUTION

Strategy and execution are often seen as two separate entities, but in reality, they are deeply interconnected. Strategy provides the roadmap for achieving long-term goals, while execution is the process of turning that strategy into action. Without a well-defined strategy, execution becomes aimless, and without effective execution, even the best strategy will fail to deliver results. In this section, we will explore the crucial role that strategy plays in the execution process and how it can drive success.

The Alignment of Strategy and Execution

Successful execution requires a clear understanding of the strategic objectives and how they align with the overall vision of the organization. Strategy provides the guiding principles and direction for execution, ensuring that every action taken is purposeful and contributes to the desired outcomes. When strategy and execution are aligned, it creates a powerful synergy that propels the organization forward.

To achieve this alignment, it is essential to communicate the strategy effectively throughout the organization. Every member of the execution team should understand the strategic objectives and how their individual roles contribute to the bigger picture. This alignment fosters a sense of purpose and ownership, motivating individuals to go above and beyond to achieve the desired results.

Strategy as a Foundation for Decision-Making

In the execution process, numerous decisions need to be made, ranging from resource allocation to prioritization of tasks. Strategy serves as a foundation for decision-making, providing a framework for evaluating options and selecting the most appropriate course of action.

When decisions are aligned with the strategic objectives, they become more focused and impactful, driving the organization closer to its goals.

Without a clear strategy, decision-making becomes reactive and ad hoc, leading to inefficiencies and missed opportunities. Strategy provides a structured approach to decision-making, considering factors such as market dynamics, competitive landscape, and organizational capabilities. By basing decisions on a well-defined strategy, organizations can make informed choices that maximize their chances of success.

Strategy as a Guide for Resource Allocation

Resource allocation is a critical aspect of execution, as it determines how effectively an organization can utilize its available resources to achieve its strategic objectives. Strategy plays a vital role in resource allocation by providing a framework for prioritizing investments and allocating resources to the most critical areas. It helps organizations identify the key areas where resources should be concentrated to drive the desired outcomes.

By aligning resource allocation with the strategic objectives, organizations can ensure that resources are deployed in a way that maximizes their impact. This strategic approach to resource allocation helps organizations avoid spreading themselves too thin and enables them to focus their efforts on the areas that will yield the greatest returns.

Strategy as a Source of Adaptability

In today's rapidly changing business environment, adaptability is crucial for successful execution. Strategy provides a foundation for adaptability by defining the organization's core purpose and values. It serves as a compass that guides decision-making and actions, even in the face of uncertainty and change.

When strategy is deeply ingrained in the organization's culture, it empowers individuals to make agile decisions that are in line with the strategic objectives. It enables organizations to respond quickly to market shifts, seize new opportunities, and navigate challenges effectively. Strategy provides a sense of direction and stability, even in turbulent times, allowing organizations to stay focused on their long-term goals while adapting their tactics as needed.

Strategy as a Driver of Accountability

Execution requires a high level of accountability at all levels of the organization. Strategy plays a crucial role in fostering accountability by clearly defining the expected outcomes and the metrics for measuring success. It provides a framework for setting goals, tracking progress, and holding individuals and teams accountable for their performance.

When strategy is effectively communicated and understood, it creates a shared sense of responsibility and ownership. Individuals become more engaged and committed to achieving the strategic objectives, knowing that their contributions are essential for the organization's success. Strategy-driven accountability ensures that everyone is working towards a common goal, fostering collaboration and synergy within the execution team.

Strategy and execution are not separate entities but rather two sides of the same coin. Strategy provides the foundation and direction for execution, guiding decision-making, resource allocation, adaptability, and accountability. By recognizing the crucial role of strategy in execution, organizations can bridge the gap between planning and implementation, driving success and achieving their long-term goals.

3. THE BLUEPRINT FOR STRATEGIC EXECUTION

3.1 CREATING AN EXECUTION PLAN

Creating an execution plan is a crucial step in the strategic execution process. It serves as a roadmap that outlines the specific actions and steps required to achieve strategic objectives. Without a well-defined execution plan, even the most brilliant strategies can fail to materialize. In this section, we will explore the key elements of creating an effective execution plan.

Understanding the Purpose of an Execution Plan

An execution plan serves as a guide that translates strategic objectives into actionable steps. It provides clarity and direction to the execution team, ensuring that everyone is aligned and working towards a common goal. The plan outlines the tasks, timelines, responsibilities, and resources required for successful execution.

The primary purpose of an execution plan is to break down the strategic objectives into manageable and measurable tasks. It helps in identifying potential roadblocks, allocating resources effectively, and monitoring progress throughout the execution process. By having a well-defined plan, organizations can enhance their chances of successful execution and achieve their desired outcomes.

Key Components of an Execution Plan

Strategic Objectives: The execution plan should clearly articulate the strategic objectives that need to be achieved. These objectives should be specific, measurable, achievable, relevant, and time-bound (SMART). By setting clear objectives, the execution team can focus their efforts and measure progress effectively.

Actionable Strategies: The execution plan should outline the specific strategies and initiatives that will be implemented to achieve the strategic objectives. These strategies should be aligned with the overall strategic direction of the organization and address the key challenges and opportunities identified during the strategy development phase.

Tasks and Milestones: The plan should break down the strategies into actionable tasks and milestones. Each task should have a clear description, assigned responsibility, and deadline for completion. Milestones serve as checkpoints to assess progress and ensure that the execution is on track.

Resource Allocation: The execution plan should identify the resources required for successful implementation. This includes human resources, financial resources, technology, and any other necessary assets. By allocating resources effectively, organizations can optimize their execution efforts and minimize potential bottlenecks.

Timeline and Deadlines: The plan should include a realistic timeline that outlines the start and end dates for each task and milestone. Deadlines should be set based on the complexity of the task, resource availability, and dependencies. It is essential to ensure that the timeline allows for flexibility and accounts for any unforeseen challenges or delays.

Risk Assessment and Mitigation: The execution plan should include a comprehensive assessment of potential risks and challenges that may arise during the execution process. By identifying these risks in advance, organizations can develop mitigation strategies to minimize their impact on the execution. This may involve contingency plans, alternative approaches, or additional resource allocation.

Communication and Reporting: Effective communication is crucial for successful execution. The plan should outline the communication channels, frequency, and stakeholders involved in the execution process. Regular reporting mechanisms should be established to track progress, identify issues, and provide updates to key stakeholders.

Developing an Execution Plan

Developing an execution plan requires a collaborative effort involving key stakeholders and the execution team. Here are the steps involved in creating an effective execution plan:

Review the Strategic Objectives: Start by reviewing the strategic objectives and ensuring that they are clear, specific, and aligned with the overall organizational strategy.

Identify Key Strategies and Initiatives: Identify the key strategies and initiatives that will be implemented to achieve the strategic objectives. These strategies should address the critical success factors identified during the strategy development phase.

Break Down Strategies into Tasks and Milestones: Break down each strategy into actionable tasks and milestones. Assign responsibilities and set realistic deadlines for each task.

Allocate Resources: Identify the resources required for successful execution. This includes human resources, financial resources, technology, and any other necessary assets. Ensure that resources are allocated effectively to avoid bottlenecks.

Assess Risks and Develop Mitigation Strategies: Conduct a comprehensive risk assessment and develop mitigation strategies to address potential challenges. This may involve contingency plans, alternative approaches, or additional resource allocation.

Establish Communication and Reporting Mechanisms: Define the communication channels, frequency, and stakeholders involved in the execution process. Establish regular reporting mechanisms to track progress, identify issues, and provide updates to key stakeholders.

Monitor and Adjust: Continuously monitor the execution progress and make necessary adjustments as required. Regularly review the plan and update it based on changing circumstances or new insights.

By following these steps and developing a well-defined execution plan, organizations can enhance their chances of successful execution and achieve their strategic objectives. The execution plan serves as a roadmap that guides the execution team towards the desired outcomes, ensuring that strategies are translated into tangible results.

3.2 SETTING CLEAR GOALS AND OBJECTIVES

Setting clear goals and objectives is a crucial step in the strategic execution process. Without clear goals, it becomes challenging to align efforts, measure progress, and ultimately achieve success. In this section, we will explore the importance of setting clear goals and objectives and provide practical guidance on how to do so effectively.

The Importance of Clear Goals and Objectives

Clear goals and objectives serve as the guiding light for strategic execution. They provide a sense of direction and purpose, helping individuals and teams understand what needs to be accomplished and why. Here are some key reasons why setting clear goals and objectives is essential:

Alignment: Clear goals ensure that everyone is on the same page and working towards a common objective. When goals are well-defined, individuals and teams can align their efforts, resources, and strategies to achieve them.

Focus: Clear goals help individuals and teams prioritize their tasks and activities. By knowing what needs to be accomplished, they can concentrate their efforts on the most critical areas, avoiding distractions and unnecessary work.

Motivation: Clear goals provide a sense of purpose and motivation. When individuals understand the significance of their work and how it contributes to the overall objectives, they are more likely to stay engaged, committed, and motivated.

Measurement: Clear goals enable effective measurement and evaluation of progress. By defining specific, measurable, achievable, relevant, and time-bound (SMART) goals, it becomes easier to track performance, identify areas for improvement, and celebrate successes.

Guidelines for Setting Clear Goals and Objectives

To set clear goals and objectives, it is essential to follow a structured approach. Here are some guidelines to help you in the process:

Start with the Vision: Begin by clarifying the organization's vision and long-term objectives. The goals you set should align with this overarching vision and contribute to its realization.

Be Specific: Clearly define what you want to achieve. Vague or ambiguous goals can lead to confusion and lack of focus. Use specific language and quantify your goals whenever possible.

Make Them Measurable: Ensure that your goals are measurable so that progress can be tracked and evaluated. Identify key performance indicators (KPIs) or metrics that will help you assess your progress towards the goals.

Set Achievable Goals: While it is important to set ambitious goals, they should also be realistic and attainable. Consider the available resources, capabilities, and constraints when setting goals to ensure they are within reach.

Relevance and Alignment: Ensure that your goals are relevant to the overall strategy and align with the organization's priorities. Goals that are not aligned can lead to wasted efforts and misalignment of resources.

Time-Bound: Set clear deadlines or timeframes for achieving your goals. This helps create a sense of urgency and provides a timeline for tracking progress.

Break Down Goals into Objectives: Break down your goals into smaller, actionable objectives. This makes them more manageable and allows for a step-by-step approach towards achieving the larger goal.

Communicate and Involve Stakeholders: Share your goals and objectives with relevant stakeholders, including team members, leaders, and other key individuals. Seek their input and ensure that there is a shared understanding of the goals and their importance.

Regularly Review and Update: Goals and objectives should not be set in stone. Regularly review and update them as needed to reflect changes in the business environment, priorities, or strategies.

Celebrate Milestones and Successes: Recognize and celebrate milestones and successes along the way. This helps maintain motivation and momentum throughout the execution process.

By following these guidelines, you can set clear goals and objectives that provide a solid foundation for successful strategic execution. Remember that goal setting is an iterative process, and it is essential to regularly review and adjust goals as needed to stay aligned with the evolving needs of the organization.

In the next section, we will explore the process of developing actionable strategies that support the achievement of your goals and objectives.

3.3 DEVELOPING ACTIONABLE STRATEGIES

In the previous sections, we discussed the importance of creating an execution plan and setting clear goals and objectives. Now, let's dive into the process of developing actionable strategies that will drive your execution forward.

Understanding the Role of Strategies in Execution

Strategies are the specific actions and approaches you will take to achieve your strategic objectives. They provide a roadmap for how you will allocate resources, make decisions, and overcome challenges along the way. Developing effective strategies is crucial for successful execution because they guide your team's efforts and ensure alignment with your overall goals.

To develop actionable strategies, you need to consider several key factors:

1. Analyzing the Current Situation

Before developing strategies, it's essential to assess your current situation. This involves analyzing your strengths, weaknesses, opportunities, and threats (SWOT analysis) and understanding the external factors that may impact your execution. By gaining a comprehensive understanding of your organization's internal and external environment, you can identify areas where strategic actions are needed.

2. Defining Strategic Priorities

Once you have a clear understanding of your

current situation, you can define your strategic priorities. Strategic priorities are the areas or objectives that are most critical to your organization's success. These priorities should align with your overall strategic objectives and provide a clear focus for your strategies. By prioritizing your efforts, you can allocate resources effectively and ensure that your strategies have the greatest impact.

3. Generating Strategic Options

With your strategic priorities in mind, it's time to generate strategic options. This involves brainstorming and exploring different approaches and actions that can help you achieve your objectives. Encourage creativity and diverse perspectives during this process to generate a wide range of ideas. Remember, not all options will be feasible or effective, so it's important to evaluate and refine them later.

4. Evaluating and Selecting Strategies

Once you have a list of potential strategies, it's time to evaluate and select the most promising ones. Consider the feasibility, potential impact, and alignment with your strategic priorities when evaluating each strategy. It's also important to assess the risks and challenges associated with each option. By carefully evaluating and selecting strategies, you can ensure that your efforts are focused on the most effective and achievable actions.

5. Developing Action Plans
Once you have selected your strategies, it's time to develop action plans. Action plans outline the specific steps, timelines, and responsibilities for implementing each strategy. They break down the strategies into actionable tasks and provide a clear roadmap for execution. When developing action plans, consider the resources and capabilities required for each task and ensure that they are realistic and achievable.

6. Communicating and Aligning
Effective communication and alignment are crucial for successful execution. Once you have developed your strategies and action plans, it's important to communicate them clearly to your execution team. Ensure that everyone understands their roles, responsibilities, and the overall strategic direction. By fostering alignment and understanding, you can ensure that everyone is working towards the same goals and objectives.

7. Monitoring and Adjusting
Execution is an iterative process, and it's important to continuously monitor and adjust your strategies as needed. Regularly track the progress of your execution efforts and evaluate the effectiveness of your strategies. If you encounter challenges or changes in the external

environment, be prepared to adjust your strategies accordingly. By staying agile and adaptable, you can ensure that your strategies remain relevant and effective throughout the execution process.

Developing actionable strategies is a critical step in the strategic execution process. By analyzing the current situation, defining strategic priorities, generating options, evaluating and selecting strategies, developing action plans, communicating and aligning, and monitoring and adjusting, you can create a roadmap for successful execution. Remember, strategies should be flexible and adaptable, allowing you to navigate challenges and seize opportunities along the way. With well-developed and actionable strategies, you can bridge the gap between strategy and successful implementation.

3.4 BUILDING A HIGH-PERFORMING EXECUTION TEAM

Building a high-performing execution team is crucial for the successful implementation of any strategic plan. A team that is aligned, motivated, and capable of executing the strategy effectively can make all the difference in achieving desired outcomes. In this section, we will explore the key elements of building a high-performing execution team and provide practical strategies for assembling and developing such a team.

The Importance of Team Dynamics

Team dynamics play a significant role in the success of strategic execution. A cohesive and collaborative team can overcome challenges, adapt to changes, and drive results. On the other hand, a team with poor dynamics can hinder progress and create roadblocks. Therefore, it is essential to focus on fostering a positive team environment and establishing clear expectations from the outset.

Assembling the Right Team

To build a high-performing execution team, it is crucial to assemble individuals with the right skills, expertise, and mindset. Here are some key considerations when selecting team members:

Diverse Skill Sets: Look for individuals with a diverse range of skills and experiences that align with the requirements of the strategic plan. This diversity will bring different perspectives and enhance problem-solving capabilities.

Collaborative Mindset: Seek team members who are willing to collaborate, share knowledge, and work towards a common goal. A team that values collaboration fosters innovation and creativity.

Leadership Potential: Identify individuals who

demonstrate leadership potential within the team. These individuals can help drive the execution process, motivate others, and take ownership of their responsibilities.

Cultural Fit: Consider the cultural fit of potential team members. A team that shares common values and beliefs is more likely to work well together and support each other during challenging times.

Developing Team Cohesion

Once the team is assembled, it is essential to focus on developing team cohesion. Cohesion refers to the degree of unity, trust, and collaboration within the team. Here are some strategies to foster team cohesion:

Establish Clear Roles and Responsibilities: Clearly define the roles and responsibilities of each team member to avoid confusion and promote accountability.

Encourage Open Communication: Create an environment where team members feel comfortable expressing their ideas, concerns, and feedback. Encourage active listening and open dialogue to foster trust and collaboration.

Promote Trust and Respect: Emphasize the importance of trust and respect within the team. Encourage team members to support and rely on each other, fostering a sense of camaraderie.

Celebrate Successes: Recognize and celebrate

team achievements to boost morale and reinforce a sense of accomplishment. This can be done through team-wide acknowledgments, rewards, or team-building activities.

Developing Team Skills and Capabilities

To ensure the team is equipped with the necessary skills and capabilities to execute the strategy effectively, it is essential to invest in their development. Here are some strategies to develop team skills and capabilities:

Training and Development: Identify skill gaps within the team and provide targeted training and development opportunities. This can include workshops, seminars, online courses, or mentoring programs.

Cross-Functional Exposure: Encourage team members to gain exposure to different areas of the organization or industry. This exposure can broaden their perspectives and enhance their problem-solving abilities.

Knowledge Sharing: Facilitate knowledge sharing within the team by creating platforms or processes for sharing best practices, lessons learned, and industry insights. This can be done through regular team meetings, knowledge-sharing sessions, or online collaboration tools.

Continuous Learning Culture: Foster a culture of continuous learning within the team. Encourage team members to stay updated with industry trends, new technologies, and best practices. This can be achieved through ongoing learning opportunities, such as lunch and learn sessions or book clubs.

Empowering the Team

Empowering the execution team is crucial for their motivation and engagement. When team members feel empowered, they take ownership of their responsibilities and are more likely to go above and beyond to achieve success. Here are some strategies to empower the team:

Delegate Authority: Delegate decision-making authority to team members whenever possible. This not only lightens the load on leaders but also empowers team members to take ownership of their work.

Provide Autonomy: Trust team members to make decisions and take initiative. Avoid micromanagement and provide them with the autonomy to execute their tasks in their own way.

Recognize and Reward: Acknowledge and reward team members for their contributions and achievements. This can be done through verbal recognition, performance-based bonuses, or career advancement opportunities.

Encourage Innovation: Create an environment that encourages innovation and experimentation. Provide team members with the freedom to explore new ideas and approaches, even if they involve some level of risk.

By focusing on building a high-performing execution team, organizations can significantly increase their chances of successfully implementing their strategic plans. A team that is aligned, motivated, and equipped with the necessary skills and capabilities can overcome challenges, adapt to changes, and drive results.

4. EFFECTIVE PROJECT MANAGEMENT

4.1 UNDERSTANDING PROJECT MANAGEMENT PRINCIPLES

Project management is a critical component of effective strategic execution. It provides a structured approach to planning, organizing, and controlling the resources and activities required to achieve project goals. In this section, we will explore the fundamental principles of project management and how they contribute to successful execution.

The Importance of Project Management

Project management is essential for ensuring that strategic initiatives are executed efficiently and effectively. It provides a framework for managing the complexities of projects, including defining objectives, allocating resources, and monitoring progress. Without proper project management, organizations risk encountering delays, cost overruns, and a lack of alignment with strategic goals.

One of the key benefits of project management is its ability to provide clarity and structure. By breaking down complex initiatives into manageable tasks and establishing clear timelines and responsibilities, project management enables teams to work towards a common goal with a shared understanding of expectations.

The Project Management Life Cycle

The project management life cycle consists of several phases that guide the progression of a project from initiation to completion. While specific methodologies may vary, the core phases typically include:

Initiation: This phase involves defining the project's objectives, scope, and stakeholders. It also includes conducting a feasibility study to assess the project's viability and potential risks.

Planning: During the planning phase, project managers develop a detailed project plan that outlines the tasks, timelines, resources, and budget required to achieve the project's objectives. This phase also involves identifying potential risks and developing strategies to mitigate them.

Execution: The execution phase is where the project plan is put into action. Project managers coordinate resources, assign tasks, and monitor progress to ensure that the project stays on track. Effective communication and collaboration are crucial during this phase to keep all stakeholders informed and engaged.

Monitoring and Control: In this phase, project managers track the project's progress, compare it against the project plan, and make adjustments as necessary. They also monitor key performance indicators (KPIs) to assess the project's performance and identify any deviations from the plan.

Closure: The closure phase involves wrapping up the project, documenting lessons learned, and conducting a post-project review. This phase ensures that the project's outcomes are delivered, and any remaining tasks or documentation are completed.

Key Project Management Principles

To effectively manage projects, it is essential to understand and apply key project management principles. Here are some fundamental principles that can contribute to successful project execution:

Clear Objectives: Clearly defining project

objectives is crucial for guiding the project's direction and ensuring that all stakeholders have a shared understanding of what needs to be achieved.

Scope Management: Managing the project's scope involves defining and controlling what is included and excluded from the project. Scope creep, which refers to uncontrolled changes or additions to the project scope, can lead to delays and cost overruns.

Effective Communication: Open and effective communication is vital for project success. Project managers must establish clear lines of communication, facilitate collaboration among team members, and ensure that stakeholders are kept informed throughout the project life cycle.

Risk Management: Identifying and managing risks is essential to minimize potential disruptions to the project. Project managers should conduct risk assessments, develop mitigation strategies, and regularly monitor and address any emerging risks.

Resource Management: Efficiently allocating and managing resources, including personnel, equipment, and budget, is critical for project success. Project managers must ensure that resources are utilized effectively and that any constraints are addressed promptly.

Quality Assurance: Implementing quality assurance processes helps ensure that project deliverables meet the required standards. This includes establishing quality control measures, conducting regular inspections, and addressing any issues or defects promptly.

Change Management: Projects often encounter changes, whether in requirements, scope, or external factors. Effective change management involves assessing the impact of changes, communicating them to stakeholders, and implementing them in a controlled manner.

By adhering to these principles, project managers can enhance their ability to execute projects successfully and achieve desired outcomes.

Project Management Methodologies

Various project management methodologies and frameworks exist to guide project execution. Some popular methodologies include:

Waterfall: The waterfall methodology follows a sequential approach, where each phase is completed before moving on to the next. This methodology is suitable for projects with well-defined requirements and minimal changes expected.

Agile: Agile methodologies, such as Scrum and Kanban, emphasize flexibility, collaboration, and iterative development. Agile is particularly useful for projects with evolving requirements and a need for frequent feedback and adaptation.

Critical Path Method (CPM): CPM is a technique

used to identify the critical path, which is the sequence of activities that determines the project's overall duration. It helps project managers prioritize tasks and allocate resources effectively.

PRINCE2: PRINCE2 (Projects IN Controlled Environments) is a process-based methodology that provides a structured approach to project management. It focuses on dividing projects into manageable stages and emphasizes continuous monitoring and control.

The choice of methodology depends on the project's characteristics, organizational culture, and stakeholder preferences. Project managers should select and tailor the methodology that best aligns with the project's requirements and objectives.

Understanding project management principles is essential for mastering strategic execution. By following a structured project management approach, organizations can effectively plan, execute, and control projects, ensuring that they align with strategic objectives and deliver desired outcomes. Clear objectives, effective communication, risk management, and resource allocation are among the key principles that contribute to successful project execution. Additionally, selecting the appropriate project management methodology can further enhance project outcomes.

4.2 PLANNING AND SCHEDULING

Planning and scheduling are critical components of effective project management. In this section, we will explore the importance of careful planning and how to create a well-structured schedule that ensures the successful execution of your strategic initiatives.

The Importance of Planning

Planning is the foundation upon which successful execution is built. It involves defining the scope of the project, setting clear objectives, and determining the necessary resources and timelines. Without proper planning, projects can quickly become disorganized, leading to missed deadlines, budget overruns, and a lack of alignment with strategic goals.

One of the key benefits of planning is that it allows you to anticipate potential challenges and develop strategies to overcome them. By considering various scenarios and developing contingency plans, you can minimize the impact of unexpected events and keep your project on track.

Creating a Project Plan

A project plan serves as a roadmap for the execution of your strategic initiatives. It outlines the tasks, milestones, and deliverables required to achieve your objectives. When creating a project plan, consider the following steps:

Define the project scope: Clearly articulate the goals, objectives, and deliverables of your project. This will help you establish boundaries and ensure that everyone involved has a shared understanding of what needs to be accomplished.

Identify the tasks and dependencies: Break down the project into smaller, manageable tasks. Determine the sequence in which these tasks need to be completed and identify any dependencies between them. This will help you understand the critical path of your project and allocate resources effectively.

Estimate time and resources: Assign time estimates to each task and determine the resources required to complete them. Consider factors such as the availability of team members, equipment, and materials. This will help you create a realistic schedule and allocate resources efficiently.

Develop a timeline: Once you have estimated the time and resources required for each task, create a timeline that outlines the start and end dates for each activity. Consider any constraints or dependencies that may impact the schedule. A visual representation, such as a Gantt chart, can be helpful in illustrating the timeline and identifying potential bottlenecks.

Allocate resources: Assign team members to specific tasks based on their skills and availability. Ensure that each team member understands their responsibilities and has the necessary support to complete their assigned tasks.

Establish milestones: Break the project into key milestones to track progress and provide a sense of accomplishment. Milestones serve as checkpoints and help you evaluate whether the project is on track or if adjustments need to be made.

Identify risks and develop contingency plans: Anticipate potential risks and develop contingency plans to mitigate their impact. Consider factors such as resource constraints, technical challenges, and external dependencies. By proactively addressing risks, you can minimize their impact on the project's success.

Scheduling and Resource Management

Once you have created a project plan, it is essential to develop a detailed schedule that outlines the specific tasks, timelines, and resource allocations. Effective scheduling involves the following considerations:

Task sequencing: Determine the order in which tasks need to be completed based on their dependencies. Some tasks may need to be completed before others can begin, while others can be executed concurrently. Understanding task dependencies is crucial for efficient resource allocation and timely project completion.

Resource allocation: Assign team members, equipment, and materials to each task based on their availability and skills. Consider any resource constraints and ensure that resources are allocated optimally to avoid bottlenecks or overutilization.

Time estimation: Estimate the time required to complete each task based on historical data, expert judgment, or input from team members. Consider factors such as task complexity, resource availability, and potential risks. It is important to be realistic in your time estimates to avoid setting unrealistic expectations or creating unnecessary pressure on the team.

Critical path analysis: Identify the critical path, which is the sequence of tasks that determines the project's overall duration. The critical path represents the longest path through the project and highlights tasks that must be completed on time to avoid delaying the entire project. By focusing on the critical path, you can prioritize resources and ensure that the project stays on schedule.

Resource leveling: Balance resource allocation to avoid overutilization or underutilization. Resource leveling involves adjusting task schedules or allocating additional resources to ensure that workloads are distributed evenly. This helps prevent burnout, improves productivity, and minimizes delays caused by resource constraints.

Schedule monitoring and adjustment: Regularly monitor the project's progress against the schedule and make adjustments as necessary. Keep track of completed tasks, identify any delays or deviations, and take corrective actions to bring the project back on track. Effective communication and collaboration with the project team are crucial during this phase.

By carefully planning and scheduling your projects, you can increase the likelihood of successful execution. A well-structured project plan and schedule provide clarity, ensure efficient resource allocation, and enable effective monitoring and control throughout the execution process. Remember, effective planning is not a one-time activity but an ongoing process that requires continuous evaluation and adjustment as the project progresses.

4.3 MANAGING RESOURCES AND BUDGETS

In the previous sections, we discussed the importance of creating an execution plan and setting clear goals and objectives. Now, let's dive into the critical aspect of managing resources and budgets in order to effectively execute your strategic initiatives.

Understanding Resource Management

Resource management is the process of identifying, acquiring, and allocating the necessary resources to execute your projects and achieve your strategic objectives. These resources can include financial capital, human capital, technology, equipment, and materials. Effective resource management ensures that you have the right resources in the right place at the right time to maximize efficiency and productivity.

Assessing Resource Needs

Before you can effectively manage resources, you need to assess your resource needs. This involves identifying the specific resources required for each project or initiative. Start by conducting a thorough analysis of your project requirements, including the tasks involved, the skills and expertise needed, and the timeline for completion. This will help you determine the types and quantities of resources required.

Acquiring Resources

Once you have identified your resource needs, the next step is to acquire the necessary resources. This can involve various activities such as hiring new employees, outsourcing certain tasks, purchasing equipment or technology, or securing funding. It is important to consider factors such as cost, quality, and availability when acquiring resources. Additionally, you may need to negotiate contracts or agreements with external vendors or partners to ensure a reliable supply of resources.

Allocating Resources

Once you have acquired the resources, the next step is to allocate them effectively. Resource allocation involves assigning resources to specific tasks or projects based on their availability, skills, and expertise. It is important to consider the workload and capacity of each resource to ensure a balanced distribution of work. Effective resource allocation requires careful planning and coordination to optimize productivity and minimize bottlenecks.

Managing Budgets

In addition to managing resources, effective execution also requires managing budgets. Budget management involves planning, tracking, and controlling the financial resources allocated to your projects. It is essential to develop a detailed budget that includes all the costs associated with your initiatives, including personnel costs, equipment costs, overhead expenses, and any other relevant expenses.

Budget Planning

Budget planning is the process of estimating and allocating financial resources to support your strategic initiatives. Start by identifying all the costs associated with your projects, including both direct and indirect costs. Consider factors such as labor costs, material costs, equipment costs, and any other expenses that may arise. It is important to be realistic and accurate in your budget planning to avoid any financial constraints during execution.

Budget Tracking and Control

Once your budget is in place, it is crucial to track and control your expenses throughout the execution process. Regularly monitor your actual expenses against your budgeted amounts to identify any variances. This will help you identify potential cost overruns or savings and take appropriate actions. Implementing effective budget control measures, such as regular financial reporting and cost analysis, will enable you to make informed decisions and ensure that your projects stay within budget.

Resource and Budget Optimization

To maximize the efficiency and effectiveness of your execution, it is important to optimize your resources and budgets. This involves continuously evaluating and adjusting your resource allocation and budget allocation based on changing project needs and priorities. Regularly assess the performance and utilization of your resources and identify any areas for improvement or reallocation. Similarly, review your budget periodically and make necessary adjustments to ensure that your financial resources are allocated in the most effective and efficient manner.

Managing resources and budgets is a critical aspect of strategic execution. By effectively assessing resource needs, acquiring the necessary resources, and allocating them appropriately, you can ensure that your projects are executed efficiently. Additionally, by carefully planning and controlling your budgets, you can avoid financial constraints and optimize the use of your financial resources. Remember, effective resource and budget management are essential for successful execution and achieving your strategic objectives.

4.4 MONITORING AND CONTROLLING PROJECTS

Once a project is underway, it is crucial to monitor and control its progress to ensure that it stays on track and achieves its objectives. Monitoring and controlling projects involves tracking the project's performance, identifying any deviations from the plan, and taking corrective actions to keep the project on course. This section will explore the key aspects of monitoring and controlling projects and provide practical strategies for effective project management.

4.4.1 Establishing Project Controls

To effectively monitor and control a project, it is essential to establish project controls. Project controls are the processes, tools, and techniques used to measure and manage the project's performance. These controls provide the necessary information to make informed decisions and take appropriate actions. Here are some key project controls to consider:

Performance Measurement:

Establish metrics and key performance indicators (KPIs) to measure the project's progress and performance. These metrics should align with the project's objectives and provide meaningful insights into its success.

Project Reporting:

Implement a regular reporting mechanism to keep stakeholders informed about the project's status. This can include progress reports, milestone updates, and financial reports. Clear and concise reporting ensures transparency and facilitates effective decision-making.

Change Control:

Establish a change control process to manage any changes to the project scope, schedule, or budget. This process should include a formal review and approval mechanism to evaluate the impact of proposed changes and make informed decisions.

Risk Management:
Continuously assess and manage project risks to minimize their impact on the project's success. This involves identifying potential risks, analyzing their likelihood and impact, and developing mitigation strategies to address them.

4.4.2 Tracking Project Progress

Tracking project progress is a critical aspect of monitoring and controlling projects. It involves comparing the actual project performance against the planned performance to identify any deviations or variances. Here are some key steps to effectively track project progress:

Establish Baselines:
Before tracking progress, establish baselines for the project's scope, schedule, and budget. These baselines serve as reference points against which actual performance can be measured.

Collect Data:
Gather relevant data and information to assess the project's progress. This can include data on

tasks completed, milestones achieved, resources utilized, and costs incurred.

Analyze Variances:
Compare the actual project performance against the baselines to identify any variances. Variances can indicate deviations from the plan and may require corrective actions.

Identify Causes:
Investigate the causes of any variances to understand why they occurred. This analysis can help identify underlying issues or risks that need to be addressed.

Take Corrective Actions:
Based on the analysis of variances and their causes, take appropriate corrective actions to bring the project back on track. This may involve adjusting the project plan, reallocating resources, or revising the project scope.

4.4.3 Controlling Project Changes
During the course of a project, changes are inevitable. However, it is essential to control these changes to prevent scope creep, schedule delays, and budget overruns. Here are some strategies for effectively controlling project changes:

Change Request Process:
Establish a formal change request process that

requires stakeholders to submit change requests for evaluation and approval. This process ensures that all changes are properly assessed and their impact on the project is considered.

Impact Assessment:
Evaluate the impact of proposed changes on the project's scope, schedule, and budget. This assessment should consider the potential risks, resource requirements, and overall project objectives.

Prioritization:
Prioritize change requests based on their urgency, impact, and alignment with the project's objectives. This helps ensure that resources are allocated to the most critical changes and minimizes disruptions to the project.

Documentation:
Maintain a comprehensive record of all approved changes, including their rationale, impact, and implementation details. This documentation provides a historical reference and facilitates future project evaluations.

4.4.4 Communication and Stakeholder Engagement

Effective communication and stakeholder engagement are vital for successful project monitoring and control. Regular and transparent communication keeps stakeholders informed about the project's progress, challenges, and achievements. Here are some key considerations for communication and stakeholder engagement:

Stakeholder Updates:
Provide regular updates to stakeholders on the project's status, including progress, risks, and changes. Tailor the communication to the needs and preferences of different stakeholders, ensuring that they receive the information they require.

Issue Escalation:
Establish a clear process for issue escalation to ensure that any problems or challenges are addressed promptly. This process should define the roles and responsibilities of different stakeholders in resolving issues.

Stakeholder Feedback:
Seek feedback from stakeholders on the project's performance and their satisfaction with the project outcomes. This feedback can provide valuable insights for improving future projects and enhancing stakeholder relationships.

Lessons Learned:
Capture and document lessons learned throughout the project to identify areas for

improvement and share best practices. These lessons can inform future projects and contribute to organizational learning.

Monitoring and controlling projects is a dynamic process that requires ongoing attention and proactive management. By establishing project controls, tracking progress, controlling changes, and engaging stakeholders, project managers can effectively monitor and control projects to ensure their successful execution.

5. RESOURCE ALLOCATION

5.1 IDENTIFYING AND ASSESSING RESOURCES

In the world of strategic execution, resources play a crucial role in achieving organizational goals and objectives. Without the right resources, even the most well-crafted strategies can fall flat. In this section, we will explore the process of identifying and assessing resources to ensure their optimal allocation and utilization.

The Importance of Resource Identification

Before diving into the process of resource assessment, it is essential to understand why resource identification is a critical step in strategic execution. Resources can be broadly categorized into four main types: financial, human, physical, and intangible. Each type of resource brings unique value to the execution process.

Financial resources encompass the capital and funding required to implement strategies effectively. These resources include budgets, investments, and cash flow. Human resources, on the other hand, refer to the skills, knowledge, and expertise of individuals within the organization. They are the driving force behind the execution process.

Physical resources include tangible assets such as equipment, technology, and infrastructure. These resources provide the necessary tools and facilities to carry out strategic initiatives. Lastly, intangible resources encompass intellectual property, brand reputation, and organizational culture. These resources contribute to the organization's competitive advantage and long-term success.

By identifying and understanding the resources available to an organization, leaders can make informed decisions about resource allocation, ensuring that the right resources are allocated to the right initiatives.

The Process of Resource Assessment
Resource assessment involves evaluating the

availability, suitability, and capacity of resources to meet the organization's strategic objectives. This process can be broken down into four key steps:

Step 1: *Inventory of Resources*
The first step in resource assessment is to conduct a comprehensive inventory of all available resources. This includes identifying and documenting financial assets, human capital, physical infrastructure, and intangible resources. It is essential to gather accurate and up-to-date information to ensure a thorough understanding of the organization's resource landscape.

Step 2: *Resource Evaluation*
Once the inventory is complete, the next step is to evaluate each resource's suitability and capacity. This involves assessing the resource's alignment with the organization's strategic objectives and its ability to contribute to the successful execution of initiatives. For example, in the case of human resources, leaders may evaluate the skills, experience, and availability of individuals to determine their suitability for specific projects.

Step 3: *Resource Gap Analysis*
After evaluating the resources, it is crucial to conduct a gap analysis to identify any resource deficiencies or imbalances. This involves comparing the organization's resource

requirements with the available resources. By identifying resource gaps, leaders can take proactive measures to address them, such as hiring additional staff, acquiring new equipment, or developing partnerships.

Step 4: *Resource Prioritization*
The final step in resource assessment is prioritizing resources based on their strategic importance and impact on execution success. Not all resources are created equal, and some may have a more significant influence on achieving strategic objectives than others. By prioritizing resources, leaders can allocate them effectively, ensuring that the most critical resources are dedicated to high-priority initiatives.

Tools and Techniques for Resource Assessment

Several tools and techniques can aid in the process of resource assessment. These include:

Resource Mapping
Resource mapping involves visually representing the organization's resources, their interdependencies, and their alignment with strategic objectives. This technique provides a holistic view of the resource landscape, enabling leaders to identify potential bottlenecks or areas of resource surplus.

SWOT Analysis

A SWOT analysis can help identify the strengths, weaknesses, opportunities, and threats associated with each resource. By understanding the internal and external factors influencing resources, leaders can make informed decisions about resource allocation and utilization.

Resource Capacity Planning

Resource capacity planning involves forecasting the organization's resource needs based on projected demand and available capacity. This technique helps leaders anticipate future resource requirements and take proactive measures to ensure resource availability.

Cost-Benefit Analysis

Cost-benefit analysis is a technique used to evaluate the financial viability of resource allocation decisions. By comparing the costs and benefits associated with different resource allocation options, leaders can make informed decisions that maximize the return on investment.

Identifying and assessing resources is a critical step in strategic execution. By understanding the types of resources available, evaluating their suitability and capacity, and prioritizing them based on strategic importance, leaders can ensure optimal resource allocation and utilization.

Through the use of tools and techniques such as resource mapping, SWOT analysis, resource capacity planning, and cost-benefit analysis, organizations can make informed decisions that drive successful execution.

5.2 OPTIMIZING RESOURCE ALLOCATION

Resource allocation is a critical aspect of strategic execution. It involves the process of distributing and utilizing resources effectively to achieve strategic objectives. In this section, we will explore strategies and best practices for optimizing resource allocation to maximize the impact of your execution efforts.

Understanding Resource Optimization

Resource optimization is about making the most efficient and effective use of available resources to achieve desired outcomes. It requires careful analysis and decision-making to allocate resources in a way that aligns with strategic priorities and minimizes waste. By optimizing resource allocation, organizations can enhance productivity, reduce costs, and improve overall performance.

Assessing Resource Needs

Before optimizing resource allocation, it is essential to assess the resource needs of your execution plan. This involves identifying the specific resources required to execute each strategy and achieve the desired outcomes. Resources can include financial capital, human capital, technology, equipment, and other tangible and intangible assets.

To assess resource needs, consider the following:

Strategy requirements: Evaluate the resource requirements of each strategy in your execution plan. Determine the types and quantities of resources needed to implement each strategy effectively.

Capacity analysis: Assess the current capacity of your organization to determine if it can meet the resource needs of your execution plan. Identify any gaps or limitations that may require additional resources or adjustments to the plan.

Risk assessment: Consider potential risks and uncertainties that may impact resource availability or utilization. Anticipate any potential resource constraints or bottlenecks that may arise during execution.

By conducting a thorough assessment of resource needs, you can gain a clear understanding of the resources required for successful execution.

Prioritizing Resource Allocation
Once you have assessed resource needs, it is

crucial to prioritize resource allocation based on strategic priorities. Not all strategies and initiatives are equal in terms of their impact and importance. By prioritizing resource allocation, you can ensure that resources are allocated to the most critical and high-impact areas of your execution plan.

Consider the following approaches to prioritize resource allocation:

Strategic alignment: Align resource allocation with the strategic objectives of your organization. Allocate more resources to strategies that directly contribute to the achievement of key goals and objectives.

Impact assessment: Evaluate the potential impact of each strategy on overall performance. Allocate resources to strategies that have the highest potential for generating significant results and value.

Resource availability: Consider the availability and scarcity of resources. Allocate resources to strategies that require critical resources that may be limited or difficult to obtain.

Risk management: Allocate resources to strategies that address potential risks and uncertainties. Prioritize resource allocation to mitigate risks and ensure the successful execution of strategies.

By prioritizing resource allocation, you can focus your efforts and resources on the most critical areas, increasing the likelihood of successful execution.

Resource Optimization Strategies

To optimize resource allocation, consider implementing the following strategies:

Cross-functional collaboration: Foster collaboration and communication across different departments and teams. By breaking down silos and encouraging cross-functional collaboration, you can leverage resources more effectively and avoid duplication of efforts.

Resource sharing: Identify opportunities for resource sharing within your organization. Pooling and sharing resources can help maximize their utilization and reduce costs. For example, sharing equipment or expertise across projects or departments can lead to significant efficiency gains.

Flexible resource allocation: Build flexibility into your resource allocation process. Anticipate changes and uncertainties that may arise during execution and have contingency plans in place. This flexibility allows you to reallocate resources quickly and adapt to changing circumstances.

Technology utilization: Leverage technology to optimize resource allocation. Use project management software, resource planning tools, and data analytics to gain insights into resource utilization and identify areas for improvement.

Continuous monitoring and adjustment: Regularly monitor resource allocation and utilization throughout the execution process. Evaluate the effectiveness of resource allocation strategies and make adjustments as needed to optimize resource utilization.

By implementing these resource optimization strategies, you can enhance the efficiency and effectiveness of resource allocation, leading to improved execution outcomes.

Optimizing resource allocation is a crucial component of successful strategic execution. By assessing resource needs, prioritizing resource allocation, and implementing resource optimization strategies, organizations can maximize the impact of their execution efforts. Effective resource allocation ensures that the right resources are allocated to the right strategies, leading to improved performance and the achievement of strategic objectives.

5.3 MANAGING RESOURCE CONSTRAINTS

In the previous sections, we discussed the importance of identifying and assessing resources, as well as optimizing resource allocation to align with strategic priorities.

However, even with careful planning and allocation, resource constraints can still arise during the execution of a strategic plan. These constraints can include limitations in budget, manpower, time, or even access to certain technologies or expertise. In this section, we will explore strategies for effectively managing resource constraints to ensure successful execution.

Understanding Resource Constraints

Resource constraints refer to limitations or restrictions that hinder the availability or utilization of resources required for executing a strategic plan. These constraints can arise due to various factors, such as budget limitations, limited availability of skilled personnel, time constraints, or external factors beyond the organization's control. It is crucial to identify and understand these constraints early on to develop appropriate strategies for managing them.

Prioritizing Resources

When faced with resource constraints, it becomes essential to prioritize resources based on their criticality to the execution of the strategic plan. Start by identifying the key resources required for achieving the strategic objectives. These resources could include financial capital, human resources, technology, equipment, or any other necessary inputs. By prioritizing resources, you can allocate them more effectively and ensure that the most critical aspects of the plan receive the necessary support.

Resource Reallocation
Resource constraints often require organizations to reallocate resources from less critical areas to more critical ones. This involves a careful evaluation of existing resource allocations and making adjustments to ensure that resources are directed towards the most important strategic initiatives. It may require reassigning personnel, reallocating budgets, or reprioritizing projects. By regularly reviewing and adjusting resource allocations, organizations can adapt to changing circumstances and optimize resource utilization.

Collaboration and Partnerships
Resource constraints can sometimes be overcome through collaboration and partnerships. Organizations can explore opportunities to share resources with other entities, such as strategic alliances, joint ventures, or outsourcing certain functions. By pooling resources and expertise, organizations can overcome individual limitations and achieve their strategic objectives more effectively. Collaboration also allows for the sharing of costs, risks, and rewards, making it a valuable strategy for managing resource

constraints.

Innovation and Creativity
Resource constraints can often lead to innovative and creative solutions. When faced with limitations, organizations are forced to think outside the box and find alternative ways to achieve their goals. This could involve leveraging existing resources in new ways, adopting new technologies or processes, or finding unconventional solutions to overcome resource limitations. Encouraging a culture of innovation and creativity within the organization can help unlock new possibilities and overcome resource constraints.

Effective Communication and Stakeholder Management
Managing resource constraints requires effective communication and stakeholder management. It is crucial to keep all stakeholders informed about the resource limitations and the strategies being implemented to address them. By maintaining open lines of communication, organizations can manage expectations, gain support from stakeholders, and potentially identify additional resources or alternative solutions. Engaging stakeholders in the decision-making process can also help generate ideas and support for managing resource constraints.

Continuous Monitoring and Adaptation

Resource constraints can change over time, and it is essential to continuously monitor and adapt resource management strategies accordingly. Regularly review the allocation and utilization of resources to identify any emerging constraints or opportunities. By staying proactive and responsive, organizations can make timely adjustments to their resource management strategies and ensure that they remain aligned with the evolving needs of the strategic plan.

Case Study: *Managing Resource Constraints*

To illustrate the practical application of managing resource constraints, let's consider a hypothetical case study. Company XYZ is a small startup with limited financial resources. They have developed an innovative product and are preparing for its launch. However, due to budget constraints, they are unable to invest in extensive marketing campaigns or hire a large sales team.

To manage this resource constraint, Company XYZ decides to focus on targeted marketing efforts, leveraging social media platforms and influencer partnerships to create buzz around their product. They also prioritize building strong relationships with a select group of potential customers, providing personalized support and incentives to drive early adoption.

By creatively utilizing their limited resources, Company XYZ successfully generates significant interest in their product and achieves a high initial adoption rate. As revenue starts flowing in, they gradually expand their marketing and sales efforts, leveraging the initial success to attract additional funding and resources.

This case study highlights the importance of prioritizing resources, finding innovative solutions, and adapting strategies to overcome resource constraints. By effectively managing their limited resources, Company XYZ was able to execute their strategic plan and achieve their desired outcomes.

Managing resource constraints is a critical aspect of strategic execution. By understanding and prioritizing resources, reallocating when necessary, fostering collaboration, encouraging innovation, and maintaining effective communication, organizations can overcome limitations and achieve their strategic objectives. Continuous monitoring and adaptation are also essential to ensure that resource management strategies remain aligned with the evolving needs of the strategic plan. By effectively managing resource constraints, organizations can enhance their execution capabilities and increase the likelihood of success.

5.4 ALIGNING RESOURCES WITH STRATEGIC PRIORITIES

In the previous sections, we discussed the importance of resource allocation and managing resource constraints in strategic execution. However, it is equally crucial to align resources with strategic priorities to ensure that the right resources are allocated to the right initiatives. In this section, we will explore strategies and best practices for aligning resources with strategic priorities.

Understanding the Importance of Alignment

Alignment is the process of ensuring that the allocation of resources, including people, time, and budget, is in line with the organization's strategic priorities. When resources are aligned with strategic priorities, it enhances the chances of successful execution and maximizes the impact of the initiatives undertaken.

Without proper alignment, organizations may find themselves allocating resources to projects or activities that do not contribute significantly to their strategic objectives. This misalignment can lead to wasted resources, missed opportunities, and ultimately, failure to achieve desired outcomes.

Steps for Aligning Resources with Strategic Priorities

To effectively align resources with strategic priorities, organizations should follow a systematic approach. Here are some steps to consider:

1. Clearly Define Strategic Priorities

Before aligning resources, it is essential to have a clear understanding of the organization's strategic priorities. These priorities should be well-defined, measurable, and aligned with the overall vision and mission of the organization. By having a clear strategic direction, it becomes easier to identify the resources needed to achieve the desired outcomes.

2. Assess Resource Availability and Capability

Once the strategic priorities are defined, the next step is to assess the availability and capability of resources within the organization. This assessment should include an evaluation of the skills, expertise, and capacity of the workforce, as well as an analysis of the financial resources and technology infrastructure available.

By understanding the existing resources,

organizations can identify any gaps or limitations that need to be addressed. This assessment also helps in determining whether additional resources need to be acquired or if existing resources can be reallocated to align with the strategic priorities.

3. Prioritize Initiatives

Not all initiatives or projects will have the same level of importance or impact on the organization's strategic objectives. It is crucial to prioritize initiatives based on their alignment with the strategic priorities and their potential to deliver desired outcomes.

By prioritizing initiatives, organizations can allocate resources more effectively, ensuring that the most critical projects receive the necessary attention and support. This prioritization process should consider factors such as strategic fit, potential return on investment, and resource requirements.

4. Allocate Resources Strategically

Once the initiatives are prioritized, the next step is to allocate resources strategically. This involves assigning the right people with the necessary skills and expertise to each initiative, as well as allocating the appropriate budget and time.

Resource allocation should be based on a

thorough understanding of the requirements of each initiative and the availability and capability of resources. It is essential to strike a balance between the needs of individual initiatives and the overall resource capacity of the organization.

5. Continuously Monitor and Adjust
Aligning resources with strategic priorities is an ongoing process that requires continuous monitoring and adjustment. As initiatives progress and circumstances change, it is crucial to reassess resource allocation and make necessary adjustments to ensure continued alignment.

Regular monitoring allows organizations to identify any resource bottlenecks or imbalances and take corrective actions promptly. It also provides an opportunity to reallocate resources based on the evolving needs and priorities of the organization.

Best Practices for Aligning Resources
To enhance the effectiveness of resource alignment, organizations can adopt the following best practices:

1. Foster Collaboration and Communication
Effective resource alignment requires collaboration and communication across different departments and teams within the organization. By fostering a culture of collaboration,

organizations can ensure that resources are shared and allocated based on the overall strategic priorities, rather than individual departmental goals.

Regular communication channels should be established to keep all stakeholders informed about the strategic priorities and resource allocation decisions. This transparency helps in building trust and ensuring that everyone is working towards the same objectives.

2. Develop a Resource Allocation Framework

A resource allocation framework provides a structured approach for aligning resources with strategic priorities. This framework should outline the criteria for resource allocation, the decision-making process, and the roles and responsibilities of different stakeholders.

By having a well-defined resource allocation framework, organizations can ensure consistency and fairness in resource allocation decisions. It also helps in avoiding ad-hoc resource allocation and ensures that resources are allocated based on objective criteria.

3. Embrace Flexibility and Agility

In today's dynamic business environment, organizations need to be flexible and agile in their resource allocation practices. Strategic priorities may change, new opportunities may arise, and unforeseen challenges may emerge. Organizations should be prepared to adjust their resource allocation accordingly.

By embracing flexibility and agility, organizations can quickly reallocate resources to address emerging needs or seize new opportunities. This adaptability enhances the organization's ability to align resources with strategic priorities effectively.

4. Leverage Technology

Technology can play a significant role in resource alignment by providing tools and systems for resource planning, tracking, and optimization. Project management software, resource management tools, and analytics platforms can help organizations streamline the resource allocation process and make data-driven decisions.

By leveraging technology, organizations can gain better visibility into resource availability, utilization, and performance. This visibility enables informed resource allocation decisions and facilitates continuous monitoring and adjustment.

Aligning resources with strategic priorities is a critical aspect of successful strategic execution. By following a systematic approach and adopting best practices, organizations can ensure that the right resources are allocated to the right initiatives, maximizing the chances of achieving desired outcomes. Continuous monitoring and adjustment are essential to maintain alignment as circumstances change. By fostering collaboration, developing a resource allocation framework, embracing flexibility, and leveraging technology, organizations can enhance their resource alignment capabilities and drive successful execution.

6. MAINTAINING AGILITY IN EXECUTION

6.1 UNDERSTANDING AGILE EXECUTION

Agile execution is a mindset and approach that enables organizations to adapt and respond quickly to change and uncertainty. In today's fast-paced and dynamic business environment, traditional execution methods may not always be effective. Agile execution provides a framework that allows organizations to embrace change, iterate, and continuously improve their strategies and projects.

The Need for Agile Execution

In the past, execution plans were often rigid and inflexible, designed to follow a linear path from start to finish. However, this approach can be problematic when faced with unexpected challenges or when market conditions change rapidly. Agile execution recognizes that change is inevitable and embraces it as an opportunity rather than a setback.

Agile execution is particularly valuable in industries where innovation and speed are critical, such as technology, software development, and startups. It allows organizations to respond quickly to customer feedback, adapt to market trends, and stay ahead of the competition.

Principles of Agile Execution
Agile execution is guided by several key principles that shape its approach:

Customer Collaboration over Contract Negotiation: Agile execution emphasizes the importance of involving customers and stakeholders throughout the execution process. By collaborating closely with customers, organizations can gain valuable insights and ensure that their execution efforts align with customer needs and expectations.

Adaptability and Flexibility: Agile execution embraces change and encourages teams to be flexible and adaptable. Rather than sticking to a rigid plan, agile teams continuously evaluate and adjust their strategies and projects based on new information and feedback.

Iterative and Incremental Approach: Agile execution breaks down projects into smaller, manageable increments or iterations. This allows teams to deliver value early and frequently, gather feedback, and make necessary adjustments along the way.

Empowered and Self-Organized Teams: Agile execution empowers teams to make decisions and take ownership of their work. Self-organized teams are encouraged to collaborate, communicate, and find innovative solutions to challenges.

Continuous Learning and Improvement: Agile execution promotes a culture of continuous learning and improvement. Teams regularly reflect on their execution efforts, identify areas for improvement, and implement changes to enhance their performance.

Agile Execution Methodologies

There are several popular methodologies that organizations can adopt to implement agile execution. These methodologies provide a structured framework for executing projects in an agile manner. Some of the most widely used methodologies include:

Scrum: Scrum is an iterative and incremental framework for managing complex projects. It divides projects into short iterations called sprints, during which teams work on specific deliverables. Scrum emphasizes collaboration, transparency, and adaptability.

Kanban: Kanban is a visual framework that helps teams manage and track their work. It uses a Kanban board to visualize tasks and their progress. Kanban focuses on limiting work in progress, promoting flow, and optimizing the overall execution process.

Lean Startup: The Lean Startup methodology is specifically designed for startups and organizations focused on innovation. It emphasizes rapid experimentation, validated learning, and iterative product development. The Lean Startup methodology encourages organizations to build, measure, and learn from customer feedback to drive execution.

Extreme Programming (XP): Extreme Programming is an agile software development methodology that emphasizes collaboration, simplicity, and feedback. XP promotes practices such as continuous integration, test-driven development, and pair programming to ensure high-quality execution.

Benefits of Agile Execution

Agile execution offers numerous benefits to organizations that embrace its principles and methodologies. Some of the key benefits include:

Faster Time to Market: Agile execution enables

organizations to deliver value to customers more quickly by breaking projects into smaller iterations and focusing on high-priority deliverables.

Improved Adaptability: Agile execution allows organizations to respond quickly to changes in the market, customer needs, or project requirements. It enables teams to pivot and adjust their strategies and projects as needed.

Enhanced Collaboration and Communication: Agile execution promotes collaboration and communication among team members, stakeholders, and customers. This leads to better alignment, shared understanding, and improved decision-making.

Increased Customer Satisfaction: By involving customers throughout the execution process and delivering value early and frequently, agile execution increases customer satisfaction and loyalty.

Higher Quality Execution: Agile methodologies emphasize practices such as continuous integration, testing, and feedback, which result in higher-quality execution outcomes.

Greater Employee Engagement: Agile execution empowers teams, encourages autonomy, and fosters a culture of accountability and ownership. This leads to higher levels of employee engagement and satisfaction.

In the next section, we will explore how

organizations can adapt to change and uncertainty in the execution process and effectively implement agile methodologies. We will discuss strategies for embracing change, managing uncertainty, and building a culture of agility within the organization.

6.2 ADAPTING TO CHANGE AND UNCERTAINTY

In today's fast-paced and ever-changing business landscape, the ability to adapt to change and uncertainty is crucial for successful strategic execution. The traditional approach of rigidly sticking to a predetermined plan is no longer effective in a world where disruption and unpredictability are the norm. To master strategic execution, you must embrace agility and develop the skills to navigate through uncertainty. In this section, we will explore the importance of adapting to change, strategies for managing uncertainty, and techniques for maintaining agility in execution.

Embracing Change

Change is inevitable in any organization. It can come in the form of market shifts, technological advancements, regulatory changes, or internal restructuring. To adapt to change effectively, you must first embrace it as an opportunity rather than a threat. Change can bring new possibilities, open doors to innovation, and create a competitive advantage if approached with the right mindset.

One key aspect of adapting to change is staying informed and continuously scanning the external environment for potential disruptions. This involves monitoring industry trends, competitor activities, and emerging technologies. By staying ahead of the curve, you can proactively identify potential challenges and opportunities, allowing you to adjust your execution plans accordingly.

Managing Uncertainty

Uncertainty is an inherent part of any business endeavor. It can arise from factors such as economic fluctuations, political instability, or unforeseen events like natural disasters. While it is impossible to eliminate uncertainty entirely, you can develop strategies to manage and mitigate its impact on your execution.

One effective approach is scenario planning, where you create multiple plausible scenarios based on different assumptions and potential outcomes. By considering a range of possibilities, you can develop contingency plans and be better prepared to adapt when unexpected events occur. Additionally, fostering a culture of flexibility and open communication within your execution team can help navigate uncertainty more effectively. Encouraging team members to share their insights, concerns, and ideas can lead to innovative solutions and a more agile response to changing circumstances.

Agile Methodologies

Agile methodologies have gained significant popularity in recent years, particularly in the realm of software development. However, their principles can be applied to strategic execution in any industry. Agile methodologies emphasize iterative and incremental progress, collaboration, and adaptability. By breaking down projects into smaller, manageable tasks and regularly reassessing priorities, you can respond quickly to changes and make necessary adjustments to your execution plans.

One widely used agile framework is Scrum. Scrum involves working in short sprints, typically two to four weeks, and regularly reviewing progress and adapting plans based on feedback. This iterative approach allows for continuous improvement and ensures that execution remains aligned with evolving strategic objectives.

Building a Culture of Agility

Adapting to change and uncertainty requires more than just implementing agile methodologies. It necessitates a cultural shift within the organization. Building a culture of agility involves fostering a mindset that embraces change, encourages experimentation, and values learning from failures.

Leaders play a crucial role in shaping the culture of agility. They must lead by example, demonstrating openness to new ideas, encouraging risk-taking, and providing support for experimentation. Additionally, creating cross-functional teams and promoting collaboration across departments can enhance agility by facilitating the exchange of diverse perspectives and expertise.

To sustain a culture of agility, it is essential to establish feedback loops and mechanisms for continuous learning. Regularly reviewing and reflecting on execution outcomes, celebrating successes, and analyzing failures can provide valuable insights for future adaptation and improvement.

In conclusion, adapting to change and uncertainty is a fundamental aspect of mastering strategic execution. By embracing change, managing uncertainty, leveraging agile methodologies, and building a culture of agility, you can navigate through the complexities of the business landscape and ensure the successful implementation of your strategic objectives. Remember, agility is not just a one-time adjustment but an ongoing mindset that enables you to thrive in an ever-evolving world.

6.3   IMPLEMENTING   AGILE METHODOLOGIES

Agile methodologies have gained significant popularity in recent years, revolutionizing the way organizations approach project management and execution. In this section, we will explore the principles and practices of implementing agile methodologies to enhance strategic execution. By embracing agility, you can adapt to change, increase efficiency, and deliver value to your stakeholders more effectively.

Understanding Agile Methodologies

Agile methodologies are iterative and incremental approaches to project management and execution. They prioritize flexibility, collaboration, and continuous improvement. Unlike traditional waterfall methods, which follow a linear and sequential process, agile methodologies embrace change and allow for frequent feedback and adaptation.

At the core of agile methodologies is the Agile Manifesto, which emphasizes four key values:

Individuals and interactions over processes and tools: Agile methodologies prioritize effective communication and collaboration among team members. By fostering a culture of open dialogue and shared responsibility, agile teams can make better decisions and deliver higher-quality outcomes.

Working software over comprehensive documentation: Agile methodologies focus on delivering tangible results rather than extensive documentation. This approach enables teams to quickly respond to changing requirements and deliver value to stakeholders in a timely manner.

Customer collaboration over contract negotiation: Agile methodologies emphasize the importance of involving customers and stakeholders throughout the execution process. By actively engaging with end-users, teams can gain valuable insights and ensure that the final product meets their needs and expectations.

Responding to change over following a plan: Agile methodologies embrace change as a natural part of the execution process. Instead of rigidly adhering to a predefined plan, agile teams continuously adapt and adjust their strategies based on feedback and evolving circumstances.

Benefits of Agile Methodologies

Implementing agile methodologies can yield numerous benefits for strategic execution:

Adaptability: Agile methodologies enable teams to respond quickly to changing market conditions, customer needs, and internal dynamics. By embracing change and adapting their strategies accordingly, organizations can stay ahead of the competition and seize new opportunities.

Transparency: Agile methodologies promote transparency and visibility across the organization. Regular meetings, progress tracking, and open communication channels ensure that everyone is aware of project status, challenges, and achievements. This transparency fosters trust and collaboration among team members.

Faster Time-to-Market: Agile methodologies emphasize delivering value in shorter cycles. By breaking projects into smaller, manageable increments, teams can release features and products more frequently, reducing time-to-market and gaining a competitive edge.

Improved Quality: Agile methodologies prioritize continuous testing, feedback, and iteration. By incorporating quality assurance practices throughout the execution process, teams can identify and address issues early on, resulting in higher-quality deliverables.

Enhanced Stakeholder Satisfaction: Agile methodologies involve stakeholders throughout the execution process, ensuring that their feedback and requirements are incorporated into the final product. This collaborative approach increases stakeholder satisfaction and reduces the risk of misalignment.

Implementing Agile Methodologies Successfully

To implement agile methodologies effectively, consider the following best practices:

Start with a Pilot Project: Begin by implementing agile methodologies on a smaller scale, such as a pilot project. This allows you to test the waters, identify challenges, and refine your approach before scaling up.

Provide Adequate Training: Ensure that team members receive proper training on agile methodologies and understand their roles and responsibilities within the new framework. Training can help overcome resistance to change and ensure a smooth transition.

Foster a Culture of Collaboration: Agile methodologies thrive in environments that encourage collaboration, trust, and open communication. Foster a culture that values teamwork, encourages knowledge sharing, and supports experimentation.

Empower Self-Organizing Teams: Agile methodologies empower teams to make decisions and take ownership of their work. Encourage self-organization and provide teams with the autonomy and resources they need to succeed.

Continuously Improve: Agile methodologies are built on the principle of continuous improvement. Regularly assess your processes, solicit feedback from team members and stakeholders, and make adjustments to enhance efficiency and effectiveness.

You can enhance your organization's ability to execute strategies successfully. Embrace flexibility, collaboration, and continuous improvement to navigate the complexities of strategic execution and deliver exceptional results.

6.4 BUILDING A CULTURE OF AGILITY

In today's fast-paced and ever-changing business landscape, agility has become a crucial trait for organizations seeking to excel in strategic execution. Building a culture of agility within your organization is essential to adapt to change, seize opportunities, and stay ahead of the competition. In this section, we will explore the key principles and strategies for fostering agility in your execution teams.

Understanding the Importance of Agility

Agility is the ability to respond quickly and effectively to changing circumstances. In the context of strategic execution, it means being able to adjust plans, processes, and resources in real-time to align with evolving goals and market conditions. An agile culture enables organizations to embrace change, experiment with new ideas, and continuously improve their execution practices.

Embracing a Growth Mindset

Building a culture of agility starts with cultivating a growth mindset within your organization. A growth mindset is the belief that abilities and intelligence can be developed through dedication and hard work. Encouraging your execution teams to embrace a growth mindset fosters a culture of continuous learning, adaptability, and resilience.

Leaders should promote a safe and supportive environment where employees feel empowered to take risks, learn from failures, and explore innovative solutions. By celebrating effort, progress, and learning, rather than solely focusing on outcomes, you create a culture that values agility and encourages experimentation.

Encouraging Collaboration and Cross-Functional Teams

Agility thrives in an environment where collaboration and cross-functional teamwork are encouraged. Breaking down silos and promoting collaboration across departments and teams allows for a more holistic approach to execution. When individuals from different backgrounds and expertise come together, they bring diverse perspectives and ideas, leading to more innovative and effective solutions.

Create opportunities for cross-functional collaboration through regular team meetings, workshops, and brainstorming sessions. Encourage open communication, active listening, and the sharing of ideas. By fostering a collaborative culture, you enable your execution teams to adapt quickly, leverage collective intelligence, and make informed decisions.

Empowering Decision-Making at All Levels

Agile organizations empower decision-making at all levels, rather than relying solely on top-down directives. By distributing decision-making authority, you enable your execution teams to respond swiftly to challenges and seize opportunities without unnecessary bureaucracy.

Empower your teams by providing them with the necessary information, resources, and authority to make decisions within their areas of expertise. Encourage autonomy and accountability, allowing individuals to take ownership of their work and make decisions aligned with the organization's strategic objectives. This decentralized decision-making approach fosters agility, as it enables quick responses to changing circumstances and promotes a sense of ownership and commitment among team members.

Promoting Continuous Learning and Adaptation

Agility requires a commitment to continuous learning and adaptation. Encourage a culture of learning by providing opportunities for professional development, training, and knowledge sharing. Emphasize the importance of staying updated on industry trends, emerging technologies, and best practices in strategic execution.

Promote a mindset of experimentation and iteration, where teams are encouraged to test hypotheses, learn from failures, and adapt their strategies accordingly. Implement feedback loops and regular performance reviews to evaluate progress, identify areas for improvement, and make necessary adjustments to execution plans.

Leveraging Technology and Tools

In today's digital age, technology plays a vital role in enabling agility. Leverage technology and tools that facilitate collaboration, communication, and real-time data analysis. Project management software, communication platforms, and data analytics tools can streamline processes, enhance transparency, and provide valuable insights for decision-making.

Invest in training your teams to effectively utilize these tools and encourage their adoption throughout the organization. By leveraging technology, you can improve communication, enhance coordination, and enable faster decision-making, ultimately fostering a culture of agility.

Celebrating Success and Learning from Failure

Finally, building a culture of agility requires celebrating success and learning from failure. Recognize and reward individuals and teams who demonstrate agility in their execution efforts. Celebrate milestones, achievements, and successful adaptations to changing circumstances.

Equally important is embracing failure as an opportunity for growth and learning. Encourage a culture where failures are seen as valuable lessons and stepping stones towards success. Foster an environment where individuals feel safe to share their failures, reflect on them, and extract valuable insights that can inform future execution strategies.

Building a culture of agility is essential for organizations seeking to excel in strategic execution. By embracing a growth mindset, encouraging collaboration, empowering decision-making, promoting continuous learning, leveraging technology, and celebrating both success and failure, you can foster a culture that embraces change, adapts quickly, and continuously improves its execution practices. Embracing agility will position your organization for success in an ever-evolving business landscape.

7. CASE STUDIES OF STRATEGIC EXECUTION

7.1 SUCCESS STORIES IN STRATEGIC EXECUTION

In this section, we will explore success stories in strategic execution to gain insights and inspiration from real-world examples. These stories highlight organizations that have effectively translated their strategic plans into tangible results through meticulous execution. By examining these success stories, we can uncover valuable lessons and strategies that can be applied to our own execution efforts.

Apple Inc.: Revolutionizing the Tech Industry

Apple Inc. is a prime example of a company that has consistently demonstrated exceptional strategic execution. Under the leadership of Steve Jobs, Apple revolutionized the tech industry with groundbreaking products like the iPod, iPhone, and iPad. One of the key factors behind Apple's success was its ability to align its execution with its strategic vision.

Apple's strategic execution was characterized by a relentless focus on innovation, attention to detail, and a deep understanding of customer needs. By integrating hardware, software, and services seamlessly, Apple created a unique ecosystem that offered a superior user experience. This cohesive approach to execution allowed Apple to dominate the market and establish itself as a leader in the tech industry.

Lessons Learned:

Align execution with strategic vision: Apple's success can be attributed to its unwavering commitment to its strategic vision. By aligning every aspect of execution with their overarching goals, Apple was able to create a cohesive and impactful customer experience.

Embrace innovation: Apple's ability to consistently innovate and introduce groundbreaking products set them apart from their competitors.

Emphasizing innovation in execution can lead to significant competitive advantages.

Attention to detail: Apple's meticulous attention to detail in product design, user experience, and marketing played a crucial role in their success. Paying attention to the finer details can elevate execution and differentiate a company from its competitors.

Amazon: Disrupting the Retail Industry

Amazon's strategic execution has been instrumental in disrupting the retail industry and transforming the way people shop. Jeff Bezos, the founder of Amazon, had a clear vision of becoming the "Earth's most customer-centric company." This vision guided Amazon's execution strategy, which focused on delivering exceptional customer experiences and leveraging technology to drive efficiency.

Amazon's execution success can be attributed to its relentless pursuit of customer satisfaction, continuous innovation, and a data-driven approach. By leveraging advanced analytics and customer insights, Amazon was able to personalize recommendations, optimize supply chain operations, and provide fast and reliable delivery services. This customer-centric execution approach propelled Amazon to become one of the world's most valuable companies.

Lessons Learned:

Customer-centric execution: Amazon's commitment to customer satisfaction was at the core of its execution strategy. Prioritizing the needs and preferences of customers can drive success and loyalty.

Embrace technology and data: Amazon's effective use of technology and data analytics allowed them to optimize operations, personalize experiences, and make data-driven decisions. Incorporating technology and data into execution efforts can lead to significant improvements and competitive advantages.

Continuous innovation: Amazon's relentless focus on innovation enabled them to stay ahead of the competition. Embracing a culture of continuous improvement and innovation can drive successful execution and long-term growth.

Tesla: Revolutionizing the Automotive Industry

Tesla, led by Elon Musk, has disrupted the automotive industry through its strategic execution and commitment to sustainable transportation. Tesla's execution success can be attributed to its ability to challenge the status quo, embrace technological advancements, and create a compelling brand.

Tesla's execution strategy focused on developing high-quality electric vehicles, building a robust charging infrastructure, and creating a unique customer experience. By combining cutting-edge technology, sleek design, and a commitment to sustainability, Tesla has become synonymous with electric vehicles and has transformed the perception of electric transportation.

Lessons Learned:

Challenge the status quo: Tesla's execution success can be attributed to its willingness to challenge traditional norms and disrupt the automotive industry. Embracing a mindset of innovation and challenging the status quo can lead to breakthrough execution.

Brand differentiation: Tesla's strong brand identity and commitment to sustainability set them apart from traditional automakers. Building a unique brand and differentiating execution efforts can create a competitive advantage.

Embrace sustainability: Tesla's execution strategy aligned with its commitment to sustainable transportation. Incorporating sustainability into execution efforts can attract environmentally conscious customers and contribute to long-term success.

These success stories highlight the importance of strategic execution in achieving remarkable results. By studying these examples, we can gain valuable insights and apply them to our own execution efforts. The key takeaways include aligning execution with strategic vision, embracing innovation and technology, prioritizing customer satisfaction, and challenging the status quo. By incorporating these lessons into our execution strategies, we can increase the likelihood of achieving our desired outcomes.

7.2 LESSONS LEARNED FROM FAILED EXECUTION

In the world of strategic execution, failures can be just as valuable as successes. While success stories provide inspiration and guidance, it is equally important to learn from the mistakes and missteps of others. By understanding the lessons learned from failed execution, you can avoid common pitfalls and increase your chances of achieving your strategic objectives.

The Importance of Failure

Failure is often seen as a negative outcome, but in the context of strategic execution, it can be a powerful teacher. Failed execution attempts can reveal weaknesses in your approach, highlight areas for improvement, and provide valuable insights into what not to do. By studying failed execution cases, you can gain a deeper understanding of the challenges and complexities involved in implementing a strategy successfully.

Lack of Clear Goals and Objectives

One common reason for failed execution is a lack of clear goals and objectives. Without a clear direction, it becomes difficult to align efforts, make informed decisions, and measure progress. Failed execution cases often demonstrate the importance of setting specific, measurable, achievable, relevant, and time-bound (SMART) goals. By clearly defining what you want to achieve and when, you provide a roadmap for your execution efforts.

Inadequate Planning and Preparation

Another common pitfall in execution is inadequate planning and preparation. Failed execution cases often reveal a lack of thorough analysis, insufficient resource allocation, and poor project management. Without proper planning, execution efforts can become disjointed, inefficient, and prone to failure. It is crucial to invest time and effort in creating a detailed execution plan, identifying potential risks, and developing contingency strategies.

Lack of Alignment and Communication

Failed execution cases often highlight the importance of alignment and communication. When different teams or departments within an organization are not aligned with the overall strategy, execution efforts can become fragmented and ineffective. It is essential to foster a culture of collaboration, ensure clear communication channels, and regularly communicate the strategic objectives and progress to all stakeholders. By promoting alignment and open communication, you can increase the chances of successful execution.

Resistance to Change

Resistance to change is a significant challenge in execution, and failed execution cases often demonstrate the negative impact it can have. When individuals or teams resist change, it can hinder progress, create conflicts, and derail execution efforts. It is crucial to address resistance proactively by involving key stakeholders early in the process, providing clear explanations of the benefits of the strategy, and offering support and resources to facilitate the transition.

Ineffective Leadership

Leadership plays a crucial role in execution, and failed execution cases often reveal the consequences of ineffective leadership. When leaders fail to provide a clear vision, set expectations, and empower their teams, execution efforts can falter. It is essential for leaders to create a culture of accountability, motivate and inspire their teams, and provide the necessary resources and support for successful execution.

Lack of Adaptability and Flexibility

In today's rapidly changing business environment, adaptability and flexibility are essential for successful execution. Failed execution cases often demonstrate the consequences of rigid and inflexible approaches. It is crucial to embrace change, be open to new ideas and perspectives, and adjust execution plans as needed. By fostering a culture of agility and adaptability, you can navigate uncertainties and challenges more effectively.

Insufficient Monitoring and Evaluation

Failed execution cases often highlight the importance of monitoring and evaluation. Without regular monitoring of progress and evaluation of results, it becomes challenging to identify issues, make necessary adjustments, and learn from mistakes. It is crucial to establish key performance indicators (KPIs), track execution progress, and conduct regular evaluations to ensure that execution efforts stay on track and align with strategic objectives.

Learning from Failure

To truly benefit from failed execution cases, it is essential to approach them with a learning mindset. Instead of dwelling on the failures themselves, focus on the lessons they offer. Analyze the root causes of the failures, identify patterns or trends, and extract actionable insights that can inform your own execution efforts. By learning from the mistakes of others, you can increase your chances of success and avoid repeating the same errors.

Failed execution cases provide valuable lessons that can help you navigate the complexities of strategic execution. By understanding the common reasons for failure and learning from the mistakes of others, you can enhance your execution capabilities and increase your chances of achieving your strategic objectives. Embrace failure as an opportunity for growth and improvement, and use the lessons learned to refine your execution approach.

7.3 ANALYZING REAL-WORLD EXAMPLES

In this section, we will analyze real-world examples of strategic execution to gain insights into what works and what doesn't. By examining these case studies, we can learn valuable lessons and apply them to our own execution efforts. Let's dive into some compelling examples:

Example 1: *Apple Inc.*

Apple Inc. is a prime example of a company that has excelled in strategic execution. One of their most successful execution strategies was the launch of the iPhone in 2007. Apple not only developed a groundbreaking product but also executed a flawless go-to-market strategy. They created a buzz around the product, generated anticipation, and strategically partnered with exclusive carriers to ensure widespread availability.

Apple's execution success can be attributed to several key factors. First, they had a clear vision and set specific goals for the iPhone launch. They meticulously planned every aspect of the execution, from product design to marketing campaigns. Additionally, Apple had a highly skilled and dedicated execution team that worked seamlessly together, ensuring that the product was delivered on time and met customer expectations.

Example 2: *Blockbuster vs. Netflix*

The case of Blockbuster and Netflix provides a stark contrast in strategic execution. Blockbuster, once a dominant player in the video rental industry, failed to adapt to changing market dynamics and emerging technologies. Despite having the opportunity to acquire Netflix in its early stages, Blockbuster dismissed the potential of online streaming and clung to its traditional brick-and-mortar model.

Netflix, on the other hand, recognized the shift in consumer behavior and executed a bold strategy to disrupt the industry. They transitioned from a DVD-by-mail service to a streaming platform, investing heavily in content creation and distribution. Netflix's strategic execution allowed them to capture a significant market share and ultimately drive Blockbuster out of business.

The key takeaway from this example is the importance of agility and adaptability in strategic execution. Blockbuster's failure to embrace change and innovate ultimately led to their downfall, while Netflix's ability to execute on their vision propelled them to success.

Example 3: *Tesla Inc.*

Tesla Inc. is renowned for its innovative electric vehicles and disruptive approach to the automotive industry. Their strategic execution has been instrumental in establishing Tesla as a leader in the market. One notable example of their execution prowess is the development and launch of the Tesla Model S.

Tesla set ambitious goals for the Model S, aiming to create a high-performance electric vehicle that could compete with traditional luxury cars. They meticulously planned the production process, invested in cutting-edge technology, and built a strong supply chain to support their vision. Tesla's execution team worked tirelessly to overcome challenges and deliver a product that exceeded customer expectations.

What sets Tesla apart is their ability to align their execution efforts with their long-term strategic objectives. They have consistently focused on innovation, sustainability, and customer experience, which has allowed them to maintain a competitive edge in the market.

Example 4: *Nokia's Missed Opportunity*
Nokia's decline in the mobile phone industry serves as a cautionary tale of failed execution. Despite being a market leader in the early 2000s, Nokia failed to adapt to the rise of smartphones and the emergence of new operating systems like iOS and Android. Their execution missteps included a lack of innovation, slow decision-

making processes, and a failure to understand changing consumer preferences.

Nokia's downfall highlights the importance of staying ahead of the curve and continuously evolving in a rapidly changing business landscape. Successful execution requires a proactive approach, constant monitoring of market trends, and a willingness to take calculated risks.
Conclusion

Analyzing real-world examples of strategic execution provides valuable insights into the factors that contribute to success or failure. From companies like Apple and Tesla, we learn the importance of clear vision, meticulous planning, and a dedicated execution team. Conversely, the examples of Blockbuster and Nokia remind us of the perils of complacency and the need for adaptability.

By studying these case studies, we can identify common patterns, best practices, and pitfalls to avoid in our own execution efforts. The key is to apply these insights to our unique situations, adapting them to our specific industry, organization, and goals. Strategic execution is a continuous learning process, and by leveraging the experiences of others, we can enhance our own execution capabilities and achieve greater success.

7.4 APPLYING INSIGHTS TO YOUR OWN EXECUTION

In the previous sections, we have explored various case studies and real-world examples of strategic execution. We have learned from both successful and failed execution attempts, and we have analyzed the key factors that contribute to effective implementation. Now, it's time to apply these insights to your own execution.

Understanding Your Execution Context

Before diving into the application of insights, it is crucial to understand your unique execution context. Every organization operates in a distinct environment with its own set of challenges, resources, and goals. Take the time to assess your organization's current state and identify the specific factors that may impact your execution efforts.

Consider the following questions:

- *What are your organization's strategic objectives?*
- *What are the key challenges and constraints you face in executing your strategy?*
- *What resources are available to support your execution efforts?*
- *What is the organizational culture like, and how*

does it influence execution?
- What are the external factors that may impact your execution, such as market conditions or regulatory changes?

By gaining a clear understanding of your execution context, you can tailor your approach and strategies accordingly.

Leveraging Lessons from Case Studies

The case studies presented in this book offer valuable insights into the world of strategic execution. They provide real-life examples of both successful and failed execution attempts, highlighting the factors that contribute to each outcome. As you apply these insights to your own execution, consider the following:

Identify similarities: Look for similarities between the case studies and your own execution context. Are there any common challenges or opportunities that you can learn from?

Learn from mistakes: Analyze the failed execution examples and identify the key mistakes or missteps that led to their downfall. How can you avoid making similar mistakes in your own execution?

Emulate success factors: Study the successful execution examples and identify the key factors that contributed to their achievements. How can you replicate or adapt these success factors to your own execution?

By leveraging the lessons from case studies, you can gain a deeper understanding of the strategies and approaches that work best in your specific context.

Developing an Execution Plan

One of the fundamental steps in executing any strategy is developing a comprehensive execution plan. This plan serves as a road-map for your execution efforts, outlining the specific actions, timelines, and responsibilities required to achieve your strategic objectives. As you develop your execution plan, consider the following:

Set clear goals and objectives: Clearly define what you want to achieve through your execution efforts. Ensure that your goals are specific, measurable, attainable, relevant, and time-bound (SMART).

Break it down: Break down your execution plan into smaller, manageable tasks and milestones. This will help you track progress and ensure that you stay on track.

Allocate resources effectively: Identify the resources required for each task and allocate them effectively. Consider factors such as budget, manpower, technology, and expertise.

Establish accountability: Clearly define roles and responsibilities for each task and ensure that individuals are held accountable for their deliverables.

Monitor and adjust: Regularly monitor the progress of your execution plan and be prepared to make adjustments as needed. This will help you stay agile and responsive to changing circumstances.

By developing a well-thought-out execution plan, you can increase the likelihood of successful implementation.

Building a High-Performing Execution Team

Execution is a team effort, and the success of your execution efforts relies heavily on the capabilities and commitment of your team members. As you apply insights to your own execution, focus on building a high-performing execution team by considering the following:

Identify the right talent: Assess the skills and expertise required for successful execution and ensure that you have the right people in place. Consider both technical skills and soft skills such as communication, collaboration, and problem-solving abilities.

Foster a culture of collaboration: Encourage open communication, collaboration, and knowledge sharing within your team. Create an environment where team members feel comfortable sharing ideas, asking questions, and challenging assumptions.

Provide training and development opportunities: Invest in the professional development of your team members. Provide training and resources to enhance their skills and keep them up-to-date with the latest industry trends and best practices.

Recognize and reward performance: Acknowledge and reward the achievements of your team members. Celebrate milestones and successes to boost morale and motivation.

By building a high-performing execution team, you can harness the collective capabilities and drive of your team members to achieve your strategic objectives.

Embracing Continuous Improvement

Successful execution is not a one-time event but an ongoing process. It requires a commitment to continuous improvement and a willingness to adapt and evolve. As you apply insights to your own execution, embrace the concept of continuous improvement by considering the following:

Establish feedback mechanisms: Implement feedback mechanisms to gather insights and perspectives from stakeholders, team members, and customers. This feedback can help you identify areas for improvement and make informed decisions.

Learn from failures: Embrace failures as learning opportunities. When things don't go as planned, analyze the root causes, identify lessons learned, and make the necessary adjustments to improve future execution efforts.

Encourage innovation: Foster a culture of innovation within your organization. Encourage team members to think creatively, experiment with new approaches, and challenge the status quo.

Stay agile: Be prepared to adapt and pivot as needed. Monitor the external environment, anticipate changes, and adjust your execution strategies accordingly.

By embracing continuous improvement, you can ensure that your execution efforts remain effective and aligned with your evolving strategic objectives.

Applying insights to your own execution requires a thoughtful and deliberate approach. By understanding your execution context, leveraging lessons from case studies, developing a comprehensive execution plan, building a high-performing execution team, and embracing continuous improvement, you can increase the likelihood of successful implementation. Remember, strategic execution is not a one-size-fits-all process. Tailor your approach to your unique context and be prepared to adapt as needed. With the right strategies and mindset, you can master the art of strategic execution and achieve your organizational goals.

8. OVERCOMING COMMON EXECUTION CHALLENGES

8.1 IDENTIFYING AND ADDRESSING ROADBLOCKS

In the pursuit of strategic execution, it is inevitable that roadblocks and challenges will arise. These roadblocks can hinder progress, derail plans, and impede the achievement of desired outcomes. However, with the right mindset and strategies, these roadblocks can be overcome. In this section, we will explore the process of identifying and addressing roadblocks to ensure smooth execution of strategic initiatives.

Understanding Roadblocks

Roadblocks can take various forms and originate from different sources. They can be internal or external, tangible or intangible, and may arise from factors such as organizational culture, resource constraints, resistance to change, or unforeseen circumstances. It is crucial to have a comprehensive understanding of these roadblocks to effectively address them.

One common roadblock is a lack of alignment within the organization. Misalignment can occur when different departments or teams have conflicting priorities or when there is a lack of clarity regarding strategic objectives. This can lead to confusion, duplication of efforts, and a lack of coordination, ultimately hindering execution.

Another roadblock is resistance to change. People naturally tend to resist change, especially when it disrupts established routines or threatens their comfort zones. Overcoming resistance requires effective communication, stakeholder engagement, and a clear articulation of the benefits and rationale behind the strategic initiatives.

Resource constraints can also pose significant roadblocks. Limited budgets, inadequate staffing, or a lack of necessary skills and expertise can impede the execution process. It is essential to identify these constraints early on and develop strategies to optimize resource allocation, seek additional resources if needed, or explore alternative approaches to achieve the desired outcomes.

Uncertainty and risk are inherent in any strategic execution process. External factors such as market volatility, regulatory changes, or technological advancements can introduce unpredictability and pose challenges. It is crucial to have contingency plans, risk mitigation strategies, and a flexible mindset to adapt to changing circumstances.

Identifying Roadblocks

The first step in addressing roadblocks is to identify them. This requires a proactive and systematic approach to assess potential obstacles and risks. Here are some strategies to help identify roadblocks:

Conduct a comprehensive analysis: Perform a thorough analysis of the internal and external factors that may impact the execution process. This includes assessing the organizational structure, culture, resources, market conditions, and competitive landscape. By understanding the context in which the execution will take place, potential roadblocks can be identified.

Engage stakeholders: Involve key stakeholders

throughout the execution process. By seeking their input and perspectives, you can gain valuable insights into potential roadblocks they foresee. This collaborative approach not only helps in identifying roadblocks but also fosters a sense of ownership and commitment to the execution process.

Use data and metrics: Utilize data and metrics to monitor and evaluate the execution progress. By tracking key performance indicators (KPIs) and analyzing data, you can identify any deviations from the planned trajectory. These deviations can indicate potential roadblocks that need to be addressed promptly.

Encourage open communication: Create an environment that encourages open and honest communication. This allows team members to voice their concerns, share potential roadblocks they foresee, and propose solutions. Regular team meetings, feedback sessions, and one-on-one discussions can facilitate this open communication.

Addressing Roadblocks

Once roadblocks have been identified, it is crucial to address them promptly and effectively. Here are some strategies to overcome common roadblocks:

Develop contingency plans: Anticipate potential roadblocks and develop contingency plans to address them. These plans should outline alternative approaches, actions, and resources required to overcome the roadblocks. By having contingency plans in place, you can minimize the impact of unforeseen obstacles.

Seek collaboration and support: Engage relevant stakeholders and seek their collaboration and support in addressing roadblocks. This can involve seeking additional resources, expertise, or guidance from other departments, teams, or external partners. Collaborative problem-solving can lead to innovative solutions and a shared sense of responsibility for execution success.

Communicate and manage expectations: Effective communication is crucial in addressing roadblocks. Keep stakeholders informed about the challenges being faced, the actions being taken to overcome them, and any adjustments to the execution plan. Managing expectations and providing regular updates can help maintain trust and confidence in the execution process.

Foster a culture of agility and adaptability: Encourage a culture that embraces change, agility, and adaptability. This involves empowering team members to take ownership of their work, encouraging experimentation and learning from failures, and promoting a growth mindset. A culture that values agility and adaptability can navigate roadblocks more effectively.

Continuously monitor and adjust: Regularly monitor the execution progress and assess the effectiveness of the strategies implemented to address roadblocks. Be prepared to make adjustments and course corrections as needed. Flexibility and a willingness to adapt are essential in overcoming roadblocks and ensuring successful execution.

By proactively identifying and addressing roadblocks, you can minimize their impact on the execution process and increase the likelihood of achieving desired outcomes. Embrace challenges as opportunities for growth and learning, and approach roadblocks with a problem-solving mindset. With perseverance, resilience, and the right strategies, you can overcome roadblocks and master the art of strategic execution.

8.2 MANAGING RESISTANCE TO CHANGE

Change is inevitable in any organization, and it is often met with resistance. Resistance to change can manifest in various forms, such as skepticism, fear, and reluctance to embrace new ideas or ways of doing things. As a leader or manager, it is crucial to understand and effectively manage resistance to change to ensure the successful execution of your strategic initiatives. In this section, we will explore strategies and techniques to manage resistance to change and foster a culture of acceptance and adaptability within your organization.

Understanding Resistance to Change

Resistance to change is a natural human response rooted in our innate desire for stability and familiarity. When faced with change, individuals may feel a sense of uncertainty, loss of control, or fear of the unknown. It is essential to recognize that resistance to change is not necessarily a negative reaction but rather a reflection of people's emotional attachment to the current state of affairs.

To effectively manage resistance to change, it is crucial to understand its underlying causes. Some common reasons for resistance include:

Fear of the unknown: People may resist change because they are uncertain about how it will impact their roles, responsibilities, and future within the organization.

Loss of control: Change often disrupts established routines and processes, leading individuals to feel a loss of control over their work environment.

Lack of understanding: When individuals do not fully comprehend the reasons behind the change or the benefits it will bring, they may resist it.

Perceived negative consequences: People may resist change if they believe it will result in negative outcomes, such as increased workload, job insecurity, or reduced job satisfaction.

Cultural and organizational factors: Resistance to

change can also stem from cultural norms, organizational politics, or past experiences with unsuccessful change initiatives.

Strategies for Managing Resistance to Change

Managing resistance to change requires a proactive and empathetic approach. Here are some strategies to help you navigate and address resistance effectively:

Communicate openly and transparently: Clear and consistent communication is vital in managing resistance to change. Ensure that you communicate the reasons for the change, its benefits, and how it aligns with the organization's vision and goals. Address any concerns or questions openly and provide regular updates throughout the change process.

Involve employees in the change process: People are more likely to embrace change when they feel involved and have a sense of ownership. Encourage employee participation by seeking their input, involving them in decision-making processes, and providing opportunities for them to contribute to the change initiative.

Provide support and resources: Change can be overwhelming, so it is essential to provide the necessary support and resources to help individuals navigate through it. Offer training programs, coaching, and mentoring to help employees develop the skills and knowledge required to adapt to the change successfully.

Address concerns and fears: Take the time to listen to employees' concerns and fears about the change. Acknowledge their emotions and provide reassurance where possible. Addressing concerns head-on can help alleviate resistance and build trust.

Lead by example: As a leader, your behavior sets the tone for the entire organization. Demonstrate your commitment to the change by embracing it yourself and modeling the desired behaviors. When employees see their leaders actively embracing change, they are more likely to follow suit.

Celebrate small wins: Recognize and celebrate the achievements and milestones along the change journey. Celebrating small wins helps build momentum, boosts morale, and reinforces the positive aspects of the change.

Provide ongoing feedback and evaluation: Regularly assess the progress of the change initiative and provide feedback to employees. This feedback loop allows for continuous improvement and helps individuals understand how their efforts contribute to the overall success of the change.

Overcoming Resistance to Change: A Case

Study

To illustrate the strategies mentioned above, let's consider a case study of a manufacturing company implementing a new technology-driven production process. Initially, employees expressed concerns about job security, increased workload, and the need to learn new skills. The management team addressed these concerns by:

- Conducting town hall meetings to communicate the benefits of the new process and how it aligns with the company's long-term goals.
- Providing training programs to equip employees with the necessary skills to operate the new technology.
- Involving employees in the decision-making process by seeking their input on process improvements and addressing their concerns.
- Recognizing and celebrating the successful implementation of the new process at various stages.

By adopting these strategies, the company was able to manage resistance effectively, and employees gradually embraced the change. The new production process resulted in increased efficiency, reduced costs, and improved product quality.

Managing resistance to change is a critical aspect of successful strategic execution. By understanding the underlying causes of resistance and implementing effective strategies, leaders can create an environment that fosters acceptance, adaptability, and ultimately, successful change implementation. Remember, change is a journey, and by actively involving employees, providing support, and addressing concerns, you can navigate this journey with greater ease and achieve your strategic objectives.

8.3 DEALING WITH UNCERTAINTY AND RISK

In the world of strategic execution, uncertainty and risk are inevitable. No matter how well you plan and prepare, there will always be factors outside of your control that can impact your execution. However, it is how you deal with uncertainty and manage risk that will ultimately determine the success of your strategic initiatives. In this section, we will explore strategies and techniques for effectively dealing with uncertainty and mitigating risk in your execution process.

Embrace the Unknown

Uncertainty is a natural part of any strategic execution process. It is important to recognize that you cannot predict or control every outcome. Instead of fearing uncertainty, embrace it as an opportunity for growth and learning. By acknowledging that there will be unknowns along the way, you can adopt a more flexible and adaptive mindset that allows you to navigate through uncertainty with confidence.

Conduct a Risk Assessment

To effectively manage risk, it is crucial to conduct a thorough risk assessment. This involves identifying potential risks and evaluating their likelihood and potential impact on your execution. By understanding the risks involved, you can develop contingency plans and allocate resources accordingly. A comprehensive risk assessment will enable you to proactively address potential challenges and minimize their impact on your execution.

Develop a Risk Mitigation Strategy

Once you have identified the risks, it is important to develop a risk mitigation strategy. This involves implementing measures to reduce the likelihood and impact of potential risks. There are several approaches you can take to mitigate risk, including:

Diversification: Spreading your resources and efforts across multiple initiatives can help mitigate the impact of a single failure or setback. By diversifying your execution portfolio, you can increase your chances of overall success.

Contingency Planning: Developing contingency plans for potential risks can help you respond quickly and effectively when they occur. These plans should outline specific actions to be taken in the event of a risk materializing, ensuring that you are prepared to address challenges as they arise.

Building Resilience: Cultivating resilience within your execution team and organization can help you navigate through uncertainty and bounce back from setbacks. This involves fostering a culture of adaptability, continuous learning, and open communication, which will enable your team to respond effectively to unexpected challenges.

Monitoring and Evaluation: Regularly monitoring and evaluating your execution progress can help you identify and address potential risks early on. By tracking key performance indicators and regularly reviewing your execution plan, you can detect any deviations or warning signs and take corrective action before they escalate into significant risks.

Foster Collaboration and Communication

Effective collaboration and communication are essential for managing uncertainty and mitigating risk. By fostering a culture of open dialogue and collaboration, you can encourage your team members to share their insights, concerns, and ideas. This will enable you to identify potential risks and develop strategies to address them collectively. Regular communication and updates will also help keep everyone informed and aligned, reducing the likelihood of misunderstandings or missteps.

Stay Agile and Flexible

In the face of uncertainty, it is important to remain agile and flexible in your execution approach. This means being open to adjusting your strategies and plans as new information emerges. By regularly reassessing your execution plan and adapting to changing circumstances, you can proactively respond to potential risks and seize new opportunities. Embracing an agile mindset will enable you to navigate through uncertainty with resilience and adaptability.

Learn from Failure

Failure is an inevitable part of any execution process, especially when dealing with uncertainty and risk. Instead of viewing failure as a setback, embrace it as an opportunity for learning and growth. Analyze the reasons behind the failure, identify any gaps in your execution process, and use these insights to improve your future strategies. By adopting a growth mindset and learning from failure, you can turn setbacks into stepping stones towards success.

Dealing with uncertainty and risk is an integral part of mastering strategic execution. By embracing the unknown, conducting a risk assessment, developing a risk mitigation strategy, fostering collaboration and communication, staying agile and flexible, and learning from failure, you can effectively navigate through uncertainty and increase the likelihood of successful execution. Remember, it is not about eliminating uncertainty and risk entirely, but rather about developing the skills and strategies to manage them effectively.

8.4 BUILDING RESILIENCE IN EXECUTION

Building resilience in execution is crucial for overcoming challenges and setbacks that may arise during the implementation of strategic plans. Resilience allows individuals and teams to adapt, recover, and continue moving forward in the face of adversity. In this section, we will explore strategies and techniques to build resilience in execution and ensure the successful completion of strategic initiatives.

Understanding Resilience in Execution

Resilience is the ability to bounce back from setbacks, adapt to change, and maintain focus and determination in the pursuit of goals. In the context of strategic execution, resilience is essential because it enables individuals and teams to navigate obstacles, overcome resistance, and stay committed to the execution plan.

Resilience in execution involves several key elements:

Adaptability: Resilient execution requires the ability to adapt to changing circumstances and adjust strategies and plans accordingly. This involves being open to new ideas, embracing feedback, and being willing to make necessary changes to stay on track.

Emotional Intelligence: Emotional intelligence plays a crucial role in building resilience. It involves understanding and managing emotions effectively, both in oneself and in others. By developing emotional intelligence, individuals can better cope with stress, maintain focus, and build strong relationships with team members.

Problem-Solving Skills: Resilient execution relies on strong problem-solving skills. When faced with challenges or setbacks, individuals and teams with effective problem-solving abilities can identify root causes, develop creative solutions, and implement strategies to overcome obstacles.

Positive Mindset: Maintaining a positive mindset is essential for building resilience. By cultivating optimism, individuals can approach challenges with a solution-oriented mindset, see setbacks as opportunities for growth, and maintain motivation and determination throughout the execution process.

Strategies for Building Resilience in Execution

Building resilience in execution requires intentional effort and the implementation of specific strategies. Here are some strategies that can help individuals and teams enhance their resilience:

Develop a Growth Mindset: Embrace a growth mindset, which focuses on continuous learning and improvement. View challenges as opportunities for growth and see setbacks as temporary obstacles that can be overcome with effort and perseverance.

Cultivate Emotional Intelligence: Invest in developing emotional intelligence skills. This includes self-awareness, self-regulation, empathy, and effective communication. By understanding and managing emotions, individuals can navigate difficult situations and maintain focus and motivation.

Encourage Collaboration and Support: Foster a collaborative and supportive environment within the execution team. Encourage open communication, active listening, and mutual support. When team members feel supported, they are more likely to bounce back from setbacks and stay committed to the execution plan.

Practice Effective Stress Management: Implement

stress management techniques to cope with the pressures and challenges of execution. This may include regular exercise, mindfulness practices, time management strategies, and seeking support from mentors or coaches.

Learn from Setbacks: View setbacks as learning opportunities. Analyze the root causes of failures or setbacks and identify lessons learned. Use this knowledge to refine strategies, improve processes, and prevent similar issues in the future.

Maintain Flexibility: Embrace flexibility and adaptability in execution. Recognize that plans may need to be adjusted based on changing circumstances or new information. By remaining flexible, individuals and teams can navigate unexpected challenges and stay on track towards their goals.

Celebrate Milestones and Successes: Recognize and celebrate milestones and successes along the execution journey. This boosts morale, reinforces progress, and provides motivation to continue moving forward.

Seek Feedback and Continuous Improvement: Regularly seek feedback from stakeholders, team members, and leaders. Use this feedback to identify areas for improvement and implement changes to enhance execution effectiveness.

Building resilience in execution is essential for successfully navigating challenges and setbacks that may arise during the implementation of strategic plans. By cultivating adaptability, emotional intelligence, problem-solving skills, and a positive mindset, individuals and teams can overcome obstacles and stay committed to the execution plan. Implementing strategies such as developing a growth mindset, fostering collaboration and support, practicing effective stress management, and learning from setbacks can enhance resilience and ensure the successful completion of strategic initiatives.

9. THE ROLE OF LEADERSHIP IN EXECUTION

9.1 LEADERSHIP'S IMPACT ON EXECUTION

Leadership plays a crucial role in the successful execution of any strategic plan. It sets the tone, provides direction, and influences the overall culture within an organization. Effective leadership can inspire and motivate teams to achieve their goals, while poor leadership can hinder progress and lead to failure. In this section, we will explore the impact of leadership on execution and discuss strategies for becoming a more effective leader in driving successful outcomes.

The Importance of Leadership in Execution

Leadership is the driving force behind execution. It is the leader's responsibility to communicate the strategic vision, set clear goals and objectives, and provide the necessary resources and support for their teams. Without strong leadership, even the most well-crafted strategies can falter.

One of the key roles of a leader in execution is to create alignment. This involves ensuring that everyone in the organization understands the strategic objectives and how their individual roles contribute to the overall success. A leader must effectively communicate the "why" behind the strategy, inspiring and motivating their teams to give their best effort.

Leadership also plays a critical role in fostering a culture of accountability. When leaders hold themselves and their teams accountable for their actions and results, it creates a sense of ownership and responsibility. This accountability mindset permeates throughout the organization, driving individuals to take ownership of their tasks and deliver on their commitments.

Characteristics of Effective Leaders in Execution

Effective leaders in execution possess certain characteristics that enable them to guide their teams towards success. Here are some key traits to cultivate:

1. Visionary Thinking
Leaders must have a clear vision of where they want to take their organization. They should be able to articulate this vision in a compelling manner, inspiring others to rally behind it. A strong vision provides a sense of purpose and direction, guiding decision-making and actions throughout the execution process.

2. Strong Communication Skills
Communication is a fundamental aspect of leadership. Leaders must be able to effectively convey their expectations, provide feedback, and address any concerns or challenges that arise. Clear and open communication fosters trust and transparency, enabling teams to work collaboratively towards shared goals.

3. Emotional Intelligence
Leaders with high emotional intelligence are adept at understanding and managing their own emotions, as well as those of others. They can empathize with their team members, build strong relationships, and navigate conflicts effectively. Emotional intelligence allows leaders to create a positive and supportive work environment, which is essential for successful execution.

4. Decisiveness

In the face of uncertainty and complexity, leaders must make timely and informed decisions. They should be able to weigh the available information, consider different perspectives, and take decisive action. Indecisiveness can lead to delays and missed opportunities, hindering execution progress.

5. Adaptability
Execution rarely goes exactly as planned, and leaders must be adaptable in the face of unexpected challenges or changes. They should be able to pivot and adjust strategies as needed, while keeping the overall vision and objectives in mind. Adaptable leaders can navigate ambiguity and guide their teams towards alternative paths to success.

Developing Leadership Skills for Effective Execution
Becoming an effective leader in execution requires continuous learning and development. Here are some strategies to enhance your leadership skills:

1. Seek Feedback and Learn from Mistakes
Actively seek feedback from your team members, peers, and superiors. Embrace constructive criticism and use it as an opportunity for growth. Reflect on past mistakes and learn from them,

adjusting your approach as necessary. Continuous improvement is key to becoming a better leader.

2. Invest in Personal Development
Take the time to invest in your own personal development. Attend leadership training programs, read books on leadership, and seek out mentors who can provide guidance and support. The more you invest in your own growth, the better equipped you will be to lead others effectively.

3. Foster a Learning Culture
Create an environment that encourages continuous learning and development within your team. Provide opportunities for skill-building, offer coaching and mentoring, and celebrate learning achievements. A learning culture promotes innovation, adaptability, and growth, all of which are essential for successful execution.

4. Lead by Example
As a leader, your actions speak louder than words. Model the behaviors and attitudes you expect from your team members. Demonstrate accountability, integrity, and a strong work ethic. When your team sees you embodying these qualities, they are more likely to follow suit.

5. Empower and Delegate
Effective leaders empower their teams by

delegating authority and responsibility. Trust your team members to make decisions and take ownership of their work. Provide them with the necessary resources and support, and give them the autonomy to execute their tasks. Empowered teams are more engaged and motivated, leading to higher levels of execution success.

Leadership is a critical factor in the successful execution of any strategic plan. Effective leaders inspire, motivate, and guide their teams towards achieving their goals. By cultivating the necessary leadership skills and characteristics, you can have a significant impact on the execution process and drive successful outcomes. Remember, leadership is not just about giving orders; it is about creating a vision, fostering accountability, and empowering your team to achieve greatness.

9.2 CREATING A VISION FOR EXECUTION

In the previous section, we discussed the impact of leadership on execution and how it plays a crucial role in driving successful outcomes. Now, let's explore the importance of creating a vision for execution and how it can guide your team towards achieving strategic objectives.

The Power of Vision

A vision serves as a guiding light, providing clarity

and direction to your execution efforts. It is a compelling picture of the future state you aim to achieve through your strategic initiatives. A well-crafted vision inspires and motivates your team, aligning their efforts towards a common goal.

When creating a vision for execution, it is essential to consider the following elements:

1. Clarity
A clear vision leaves no room for ambiguity. It should clearly articulate what success looks like and provide a vivid description of the desired outcome. By painting a clear picture, you enable your team to understand the destination and align their actions accordingly.

2. Alignment with Strategy
Your vision for execution should be closely aligned with your overall strategic objectives. It should reflect the strategic priorities and goals set forth in your strategic plan. This alignment ensures that your execution efforts are focused on driving the desired outcomes and moving the organization closer to its strategic vision.

3. Inspirational and Motivating
A compelling vision should inspire and motivate your team. It should ignite a sense of purpose and create a shared sense of excitement and enthusiasm. By connecting the vision to the larger

purpose of the organization, you can tap into the intrinsic motivation of your team members, driving their commitment and dedication.

4. Realistic and Attainable

While it is important for your vision to be ambitious, it should also be realistic and attainable. Setting unrealistic expectations can lead to frustration and demotivation. By ensuring that your vision is within reach, you create a sense of belief and confidence within your team, fostering a positive and can-do attitude.

Communicating the Vision

Creating a vision for execution is only the first step. To make it truly impactful, you must effectively communicate it to your team. Communication plays a vital role in ensuring that everyone understands and embraces the vision, aligning their efforts towards its realization.

Here are some key considerations for effectively communicating your vision:

1. Be Clear and Concise

When communicating your vision, be clear and concise in your messaging. Use simple and straightforward language that is easily understood by all. Avoid jargon or technical terms that may confuse or alienate team members. The more accessible your message, the better it will resonate with your team.

2. Use Multiple Channels
Utilize multiple communication channels to ensure that your message reaches everyone. Consider using a combination of team meetings, emails, presentations, and other mediums that are accessible to all team members. By diversifying your communication channels, you increase the likelihood of your message being received and understood.

3. Tell a Compelling Story
Craft a compelling narrative around your vision. Use storytelling techniques to engage your team emotionally and intellectually. A well-told story can capture the imagination of your team, making the vision more relatable and memorable. By connecting the vision to real-life examples and experiences, you can create a deeper level of understanding and buy-in.

4. Encourage Two-Way Communication
Communication should be a two-way process. Encourage your team members to ask questions, provide feedback, and share their thoughts and ideas. By fostering an environment of open communication, you create a sense of ownership and involvement. This not only strengthens the team's commitment to the vision but also allows for valuable insights and perspectives to be

shared.

Leading by Example

Creating a vision for execution is not enough; you must also lead by example. As a leader, your actions and behaviors should align with the vision you have set forth. Your team looks to you for guidance and inspiration, and your commitment to the vision will influence their level of dedication and engagement.

Here are some ways you can lead by example:

1. Demonstrate Passion and Enthusiasm

Show genuine passion and enthusiasm for the vision. Let your excitement be contagious and inspire your team members to share in your enthusiasm. Your energy and commitment will motivate others to give their best and go the extra mile.

2. Stay Focused and Aligned

Consistently demonstrate alignment with the vision in your decision-making and actions. Ensure that your priorities and initiatives are in line with the desired outcomes. By staying focused and aligned, you set the standard for the rest of the team, reinforcing the importance of the vision.

3. Celebrate Successes

Acknowledge and celebrate milestones and achievements along the way. Recognize the efforts and contributions of your team members, reinforcing the connection between their actions and the vision. Celebrating successes not only boosts morale but also reinforces the importance of the vision and the value of execution.

4. Embrace Continuous Improvement

Demonstrate a commitment to continuous improvement by seeking feedback and actively looking for ways to enhance execution. Encourage your team members to share their ideas and suggestions for improvement. By fostering a culture of continuous learning and growth, you create an environment that supports the vision and encourages innovation.

Creating a vision for execution is a critical step in driving successful outcomes. A well-crafted vision provides clarity, alignment, inspiration, and motivation to your team. By effectively communicating the vision and leading by example, you can guide your team towards achieving strategic objectives and mastering the art of strategic execution.

9.3 BUILDING A CULTURE OF ACCOUNTABILITY

Building a culture of accountability is crucial for successful strategic execution. When individuals and teams take ownership of their responsibilities and are held accountable for their actions, it creates a sense of commitment and ensures that everyone is aligned with the organization's goals. In this section, we will explore the key elements of building a culture of accountability and provide practical strategies for implementation.

The Importance of Accountability

Accountability is the cornerstone of effective execution. It ensures that individuals and teams are responsible for their actions and outcomes, and it fosters a culture of trust and transparency. When accountability is ingrained in the organizational culture, it becomes a driving force for achieving strategic objectives.

Without accountability, execution can falter. Deadlines may be missed, tasks may be neglected, and overall performance may suffer. On the other hand, when individuals feel a sense of ownership and are held accountable for their work, they are more likely to take initiative, meet deadlines, and deliver high-quality results.

Creating a Culture of Accountability

Building a culture of accountability requires a systematic approach that involves leadership, communication, and reinforcement. Here are some key steps to consider:

1. Set Clear Expectations

To foster accountability, it is essential to set clear expectations from the outset. Clearly define roles, responsibilities, and performance standards for each individual and team. Ensure that everyone understands what is expected of them and how their work contributes to the overall strategic objectives. This clarity helps individuals take ownership of their responsibilities and understand the impact of their actions.

2. Lead by Example

Leaders play a crucial role in shaping the culture of accountability. They must lead by example and demonstrate their commitment to accountability. When leaders hold themselves accountable for their actions and decisions, it sets a powerful precedent for others to follow. Leaders should also be transparent about their own successes and failures, emphasizing the importance of learning from mistakes and taking responsibility for outcomes.

3. Foster Open Communication

Open and transparent communication is vital for building a culture of accountability. Encourage individuals and teams to share progress, challenges, and ideas openly. Create a safe environment where people feel comfortable discussing issues and seeking help when needed. Regularly communicate strategic objectives, progress updates, and performance expectations to keep everyone aligned and informed.

4. Provide Support and Resources
Accountability is not just about holding individuals responsible; it also involves providing the necessary support and resources for success. Ensure that individuals have the tools, training, and resources they need to fulfill their responsibilities effectively. Offer guidance, mentorship, and coaching to help individuals overcome challenges and develop their skills. By providing support, you empower individuals to take ownership of their work and deliver results.

5. Establish Performance Metrics
Measuring performance is essential for accountability. Establish clear and measurable performance metrics that align with strategic objectives. Regularly track and evaluate progress against these metrics, providing feedback and recognition for achievements. Performance metrics provide a tangible way to assess accountability and identify areas for improvement.

6. Recognize and Reward Accountability
Recognizing and rewarding accountability

reinforces its importance within the organization. Celebrate individuals and teams who consistently demonstrate accountability and achieve their goals. Publicly acknowledge their efforts and the positive impact they have on the organization. By recognizing and rewarding accountability, you create a culture where individuals are motivated to take ownership and deliver results.

7. Address Non-Accountability
Inevitably, there may be instances where individuals or teams fail to meet their responsibilities. It is crucial to address non-accountability promptly and constructively. Provide feedback and guidance to help individuals understand the impact of their actions and identify ways to improve. If necessary, implement appropriate consequences for repeated non-accountability. By addressing non-accountability, you reinforce the importance of taking ownership and ensure that everyone is committed to the organization's success.

Building a culture of accountability is a fundamental aspect of successful strategic execution. It requires clear expectations, leadership by example, open communication, support and resources, performance metrics, recognition and rewards, and addressing non-accountability. By fostering a culture of accountability, organizations can ensure that individuals and teams take ownership of their responsibilities, align with strategic objectives, and deliver exceptional results.

9.4 EMPOWERING AND MOTIVATING EXECUTION TEAMS

One of the key factors in successful strategic execution is the ability to empower and motivate your execution teams. As a leader, it is your responsibility to create an environment where your team members feel empowered to take ownership of their work and are motivated to give their best effort. In this section, we will explore strategies and techniques to empower and motivate your execution teams.

Creating a Culture of Empowerment

Empowerment is about giving your team members the authority, autonomy, and resources they need to make decisions and take action. When team members feel empowered, they are more likely to take ownership of their work, be proactive, and contribute to the overall success of the execution process. Here are some strategies to create a culture of empowerment:

Delegate authority: Delegate decision-making authority to your team members based on their skills, expertise, and level of responsibility. This not only lightens your workload but also shows trust and confidence in your team members' abilities.

Provide resources: Ensure that your team members have access to the necessary resources, such as tools, technology, and training, to effectively carry out their tasks. Lack of resources can hinder their ability to perform and demotivate them.

Encourage innovation: Foster a culture of innovation by encouraging your team members to think creatively, share ideas, and take calculated risks. Recognize and reward innovative solutions and initiatives to reinforce the importance of innovation.

Promote collaboration: Create opportunities for collaboration and teamwork among your team members. Encourage open communication, knowledge sharing, and cross-functional collaboration to leverage the diverse skills and perspectives within your team.

Motivating Your Execution Teams

Motivation plays a crucial role in driving the performance and commitment of your execution teams. When team members are motivated, they are more likely to go above and beyond to achieve their goals and contribute to the overall success of the execution process. Here are some strategies to motivate your execution teams:

Set clear goals: Clearly communicate the goals and objectives of the execution process to your team members. Ensure that the goals are specific, measurable, achievable, relevant, and time-bound (SMART). When team members have a clear understanding of what they are working towards, it increases their motivation and focus.

Provide feedback and recognition: Regularly provide constructive feedback to your team members on their performance. Recognize and celebrate their achievements and milestones along the way. Positive reinforcement and recognition can boost morale and motivate team members to continue performing at their best.

Offer growth opportunities: Provide opportunities for professional growth and development to your team members. This can include training programs, workshops, mentoring, or challenging assignments. When team members see a clear path for their personal and professional growth, they are more motivated to excel in their work.

Promote work-life balance: Encourage a healthy work-life balance among your team members. Recognize the importance of their personal lives and well-being. Offer flexibility in work arrangements, such as remote work options or flexible hours, to help them maintain a balance between work and personal commitments.

Lead by example: As a leader, your behavior and attitude have a significant impact on the motivation of your team members. Lead by example, demonstrate a strong work ethic, and show enthusiasm and passion for the execution process. Your positive attitude and energy will inspire and motivate your team members.

Building Trust and Communication

Trust and effective communication are essential elements in empowering and motivating your execution teams. When team members trust their leaders and feel that their voices are heard, they are more likely to be engaged and motivated. Here are some strategies to build trust and improve communication:

Be transparent: Be open and transparent in your communication with your team members. Share information about the execution process, progress, challenges, and decisions. This helps build trust and ensures that everyone is on the same page.

Listen actively: Actively listen to your team members' ideas, concerns, and feedback. Show genuine interest and empathy. This not only makes team members feel valued but also provides valuable insights and perspectives that can contribute to the success of the execution process.

Encourage open communication: Create a safe and supportive environment where team members feel comfortable expressing their opinions and ideas. Encourage open dialogue and constructive discussions. This fosters collaboration, innovation, and trust within the team.

Address conflicts promptly: Conflict can arise in any team. It is important to address conflicts promptly and effectively. Encourage open and respectful communication to resolve conflicts and find mutually beneficial solutions. This helps maintain a positive and productive team environment.

By empowering and motivating your execution teams, you create a strong foundation for successful strategic execution. When team members feel empowered, motivated, and trusted, they are more likely to take ownership of their work, collaborate effectively, and deliver exceptional results. As a leader, your role is to create the conditions for their success and provide the support they need to excel.

10. MEASURING SUCCESS AND CONTINUOUS IMPROVEMENT

10.1 DEFINING KEY PERFORMANCE INDICATORS

Key Performance Indicators (KPIs) are essential tools for measuring the success and progress of strategic execution. They provide a quantifiable way to assess whether the desired outcomes and objectives of a strategy are being achieved. In this section, we will explore the importance of defining KPIs, how to select the right ones for your organization, and how to effectively use them to track and evaluate execution progress.

Why are Key Performance Indicators important?

Key Performance Indicators serve as a compass for organizations, guiding them towards their strategic goals. They provide a clear and measurable way to assess performance, identify areas for improvement, and make informed decisions. Without well-defined KPIs, it becomes challenging to determine whether a strategy is on track or if adjustments need to be made.

KPIs also help align the efforts of different teams and individuals within an organization. By establishing common metrics, everyone can work towards a shared understanding of success and contribute to the overall strategic objectives. This alignment fosters collaboration, accountability, and a sense of purpose among team members.

Selecting the right Key Performance Indicators

Choosing the right KPIs is crucial for effective measurement and evaluation. Here are some key considerations when selecting KPIs:

Alignment with strategic objectives: KPIs should directly reflect the goals and objectives outlined in the execution plan. They should provide insight into the progress made towards achieving these strategic outcomes.

Relevance and measurability: KPIs should be meaningful and measurable. They should provide actionable data that can be tracked and analyzed over time. Avoid selecting KPIs that are too vague or difficult to quantify.

Balance between leading and lagging indicators: Leading indicators provide early signals of progress towards a desired outcome, while lagging indicators measure the actual results achieved. A combination of both types of indicators provides a comprehensive view of performance.

Focus on critical success factors: Identify the key drivers of success for your strategy and select KPIs that reflect these critical factors. By monitoring these indicators, you can ensure that the most important aspects of your strategy are being effectively executed.

Consider industry benchmarks: Research industry benchmarks and best practices to gain insights into commonly used KPIs in your field. While it's important to tailor KPIs to your specific strategy, benchmarking can provide valuable context and help set realistic targets.

Keep it simple: Avoid the temptation to track too many KPIs. Focus on a few key metrics that provide the most relevant and actionable information. This will prevent information overload and ensure that attention is directed towards the most critical areas.

Using Key Performance Indicators

effectively

Once you have defined your KPIs, it's essential to use them effectively to track and evaluate execution progress. Here are some best practices for using KPIs:

Regular monitoring and reporting: Establish a regular cadence for monitoring and reporting on KPIs. This could be weekly, monthly, or quarterly, depending on the nature of your strategy and the availability of data. Consistent monitoring allows for timely identification of issues and the opportunity to take corrective action.

Visual representation: Present KPIs in a visually appealing and easy-to-understand format. Visual representations such as charts, graphs, and dashboards make it easier to interpret data and identify trends or patterns.

Contextualize the data: Provide context and explanations for the KPIs being tracked. This helps stakeholders understand the significance of the data and its implications for the overall strategy. Contextualization also facilitates meaningful discussions and decision-making based on the KPIs.

Regular review and analysis: Regularly review and analyze the KPI data to gain insights into performance trends, areas of improvement, and potential bottlenecks. Use this analysis to inform decision-making, adjust execution plans, and allocate resources effectively.

Continuous improvement: Use KPIs as a tool for continuous improvement. Identify areas where performance is falling short of targets and develop action plans to address these gaps. Regularly reassess and refine your KPIs to ensure they remain relevant and aligned with evolving strategic objectives.

Communicate and celebrate success: Share KPI results with relevant stakeholders to foster transparency and accountability. Celebrate successes and milestones achieved, recognizing the efforts of individuals and teams involved in the execution process. This promotes a positive and motivated execution culture.

By defining and effectively using Key Performance Indicators, organizations can gain valuable insights into their strategic execution progress. KPIs provide a tangible way to measure success, identify areas for improvement, and drive continuous improvement. When aligned with strategic objectives and used in a focused and meaningful manner, KPIs become powerful tools for mastering strategic execution.

10.2 TRACKING AND EVALUATING EXECUTION PROGRESS

Tracking and evaluating execution progress is a critical aspect of strategic execution. Without proper monitoring and assessment, it becomes challenging to determine whether the execution plan is on track and achieving the desired outcomes. In this section, we will explore the importance of tracking and evaluating execution progress and discuss effective strategies for doing so.

The Importance of Tracking and Evaluating Execution Progress

Tracking and evaluating execution progress provides valuable insights into the effectiveness of the execution plan and allows for timely adjustments and improvements. Here are some key reasons why tracking and evaluation are crucial:

Identifying Deviations: By monitoring execution progress, you can identify any deviations from the original plan. This enables you to take corrective actions promptly and prevent small issues from turning into significant problems.

Ensuring Accountability: Tracking progress holds individuals and teams accountable for their responsibilities. It provides a clear picture of who is responsible for specific tasks and helps identify any bottlenecks or areas where additional support may be required.

Measuring Performance: Evaluation allows you to measure the performance of the execution plan against predefined goals and objectives. It helps you determine whether the plan is delivering the expected results and provides insights into areas that require improvement.

Facilitating Learning and Improvement: Tracking and evaluating execution progress provide valuable data for learning and improvement. By analyzing the progress and outcomes, you can identify patterns, trends, and best practices that can be applied to future execution efforts.

Strategies for Tracking and Evaluating Execution Progress

To effectively track and evaluate execution progress, consider implementing the following strategies:

Establish Key Performance Indicators (KPIs): Define specific KPIs that align with your strategic objectives. These KPIs should be measurable, relevant, and time-bound. They will serve as benchmarks for tracking progress and evaluating the success of your execution plan.

Regular Reporting and Communication: Implement a reporting mechanism that ensures regular updates on execution progress. This can include weekly or monthly progress reports, team meetings, or project management software that allows for real-time updates. Effective communication ensures that everyone involved is aware of the progress and can address any issues promptly.

Use Data and Metrics: Collect relevant data and metrics to assess execution progress objectively. This can include financial data, customer satisfaction scores, project milestones, or any other quantifiable measures that align with your strategic objectives. Analyzing this data will provide insights into the effectiveness of your execution plan.

Monitor Milestones and Deadlines: Break down your execution plan into milestones and set clear deadlines for each. Regularly monitor the achievement of these milestones and assess whether they are being met within the specified timeframes. This will help you identify any delays or bottlenecks and take appropriate actions.

Seek Feedback and Input: Encourage feedback from stakeholders, team members, and customers throughout the execution process. Their input can provide valuable insights into the progress and effectiveness of the plan. Actively listen to their feedback and make necessary adjustments to improve execution outcomes.

Perform Periodic Reviews: Conduct periodic reviews to evaluate the overall progress and effectiveness of the execution plan. These reviews can be done at predetermined intervals or at key milestones. Assess whether the plan is on track, identify any gaps or challenges, and make adjustments as needed.

Continuous Improvement: Use the insights gained from tracking and evaluating execution progress to drive continuous improvement. Identify areas where the plan can be optimized, processes can be streamlined, or resources can be better allocated. Continuously strive for excellence in execution by learning from past experiences and implementing improvements.

Remember, tracking and evaluating execution progress is an ongoing process. It requires consistent effort and attention to ensure that your execution plan remains aligned with your strategic objectives. By implementing these strategies, you will be able to effectively monitor progress, identify areas for improvement, and ultimately achieve successful execution.

In the next section, we will explore the implementation of continuous improvement practices to enhance execution outcomes.

10.3 IMPLEMENTING CONTINUOUS IMPROVEMENT PRACTICES

Continuous improvement is a fundamental aspect of strategic execution. It involves consistently evaluating and enhancing your processes, systems, and strategies to drive better results and stay ahead of the competition. By implementing continuous improvement practices, you can ensure that your execution efforts are always evolving and adapting to the changing business landscape. In this section, we will explore the key principles and strategies for implementing continuous improvement practices in your organization.

The Importance of Continuous Improvement

Continuous improvement is not just a buzzword; it is a mindset that can transform your organization. By embracing a culture of continuous improvement, you create an environment where innovation and growth thrive. Here are some key reasons why implementing continuous improvement practices is crucial:

Enhanced Efficiency: Continuous improvement allows you to identify and eliminate inefficiencies in your processes, leading to increased productivity and cost savings.

Quality Improvement: By continuously evaluating and refining your execution strategies, you can enhance the quality of your products or services, leading to higher customer satisfaction and loyalty.

Adaptability: The business landscape is constantly evolving, and continuous improvement practices enable you to adapt to changes quickly and effectively.

Employee Engagement: Involving employees in the continuous improvement process empowers them and fosters a sense of ownership and engagement in their work.

Key Principles of Continuous Improvement

To effectively implement continuous improvement practices, it is essential to adhere to some key principles. These principles serve as a guide to ensure that your efforts are focused and yield meaningful results. Here are four key principles to consider:

Customer Focus: Continuous improvement should always be driven by the needs and expectations of your customers. By understanding their preferences and pain points, you can identify areas for improvement and deliver greater value.

Data-Driven Decision Making: Base your improvement efforts on data and facts rather than assumptions or personal opinions. Collect and analyze relevant data to gain insights into your processes and identify areas for improvement.

Collaboration and Empowerment: Involve employees at all levels in the continuous improvement process. Encourage collaboration, idea sharing, and experimentation. Empower employees to take ownership of their work and contribute to the improvement efforts.

Iterative Approach: Continuous improvement is an ongoing process. Embrace an iterative approach where you make small, incremental changes and evaluate their impact. Learn from each iteration and use the insights gained to drive further improvements.

Strategies for Implementing Continuous Improvement

Implementing continuous improvement practices requires a systematic approach. Here are some strategies to help you effectively implement continuous improvement in your organization:

Establish a Continuous Improvement Team: Form a dedicated team responsible for driving the continuous improvement efforts. This team should consist of individuals from different departments and levels within the organization, ensuring diverse perspectives and expertise.

Define Clear Improvement Goals: Set specific, measurable, achievable, relevant, and time-bound (SMART) goals for your continuous improvement efforts. These goals should align with your overall strategic objectives and provide a clear direction for your improvement initiatives.

Create a Feedback Loop: Establish mechanisms to gather feedback from customers, employees, and other stakeholders. Regularly collect feedback through surveys, interviews, and other channels to identify areas for improvement and validate the effectiveness of your improvement initiatives.

Implement Lean and Six Sigma Principles: Lean and Six Sigma methodologies provide valuable tools and techniques for process improvement. Incorporate these principles into your continuous improvement practices to streamline processes, reduce waste, and enhance efficiency.

Encourage Innovation and Experimentation: Foster a culture of innovation by encouraging employees to generate new ideas and experiment with different approaches. Create a safe environment where failure is seen as an opportunity for learning and growth.

Promote Continuous Learning: Invest in training and development programs to enhance the skills and knowledge of your employees. Encourage them to stay updated with industry trends and best practices, fostering a culture of continuous learning and improvement.

Recognize and Reward Improvement Efforts: Acknowledge and celebrate the efforts and achievements of individuals and teams involved in the continuous improvement process. Recognize their contributions and provide incentives to encourage ongoing engagement and participation.

Continuous Improvement Tools and Techniques

Several tools and techniques can support your continuous improvement efforts. Here are some commonly used ones:

Process Mapping: Use process mapping techniques, such as flowcharts or value stream mapping, to visualize and understand your processes. This helps identify bottlenecks, redundancies, and areas for improvement.

Root Cause Analysis: Apply root cause analysis techniques, such as the 5 Whys or fishbone diagrams, to identify the underlying causes of problems or inefficiencies. This enables you to address the root causes rather than just the symptoms.

Kaizen Events: Conduct Kaizen events, which are focused improvement workshops involving cross-functional teams. These events aim to identify and implement quick, incremental improvements in specific processes or areas.

Benchmarking: Compare your performance against industry leaders or best-in-class organizations to identify areas where you can improve. Benchmarking provides insights into industry trends and helps set realistic improvement targets.

Plan-Do-Check-Act (PDCA) Cycle: The PDCA cycle, also known as the Deming cycle, is a continuous improvement framework that involves planning, implementing, evaluating, and adjusting improvement initiatives. It provides a structured approach to drive continuous improvement.

By implementing these strategies and utilizing the appropriate tools and techniques, you can establish a robust continuous improvement framework that drives ongoing success and growth.

In the next section, we will explore how to leverage feedback from your execution efforts to inform and improve future execution strategies.

10.4 LEVERAGING FEEDBACK FOR FUTURE EXECUTION

Feedback is a powerful tool that can significantly impact the success of your strategic execution. It provides valuable insights into what is working well and what needs improvement, allowing you to make informed decisions and adjustments to your execution plan. In this section, we will explore the importance of leveraging feedback for future execution and discuss strategies for effectively collecting, analyzing, and utilizing feedback.

The Value of Feedback

Feedback serves as a mirror that reflects the reality of your execution efforts. It provides an objective assessment of your progress, highlighting areas of strength and areas that require attention. By actively seeking and embracing feedback, you can gain a deeper understanding of your execution performance and identify opportunities for growth and improvement.

One of the key benefits of feedback is its ability to uncover blind spots. As you execute your strategic plan, it is easy to become immersed in the day-to-day activities and lose sight of the bigger picture. Feedback from various stakeholders, including team members, customers, and partners, can shed light on aspects of your execution that may have gone unnoticed. This newfound awareness allows you to make necessary adjustments and course corrections to ensure the success of your execution.

Feedback also plays a crucial role in fostering a culture of continuous improvement. By encouraging open and honest feedback, you create an environment where team members feel comfortable sharing their thoughts and ideas. This promotes collaboration, innovation, and a collective commitment to achieving excellence in execution.

Collecting Feedback
To leverage feedback effectively, you must establish mechanisms for collecting it from

relevant sources. Here are some strategies to consider:

Surveys and questionnaires: Design and distribute surveys or questionnaires to gather feedback from team members, customers, and other stakeholders. Ensure that the questions are specific, relevant, and easy to understand. Consider using a mix of quantitative and qualitative questions to capture both numerical data and subjective opinions.

One-on-one interviews: Conduct individual interviews with key stakeholders to gain deeper insights into their experiences and perspectives. These interviews provide an opportunity for more in-depth discussions and allow for the exploration of specific issues or concerns.

Focus groups: Organize focus groups consisting of diverse stakeholders to facilitate group discussions and generate collective feedback. This approach encourages participants to build upon each other's ideas and provides a broader perspective on the execution process.

360-degree feedback: Implement a 360-degree feedback process where team members receive feedback from their peers, subordinates, and superiors. This comprehensive approach provides a holistic view of an individual's performance and fosters a culture of mutual feedback and development.

Real-time feedback: Encourage ongoing feedback

through regular check-ins, progress meetings, and open communication channels. This allows for immediate course corrections and ensures that feedback is timely and relevant.

Analyzing and Utilizing Feedback

Collecting feedback is only the first step; the real value lies in analyzing and utilizing it to drive future execution. Here are some strategies to help you make the most of the feedback you receive:

Identify patterns and trends: Look for common themes and patterns in the feedback you receive. Identify recurring issues or areas of strength that require attention or further development. This analysis will help you prioritize your improvement efforts and focus on the most critical areas.

Prioritize actionable feedback: Not all feedback will be equally actionable or relevant to your execution plan. Prioritize feedback that aligns with your strategic objectives and has the potential to drive meaningful change. Focus on feedback that provides specific suggestions or identifies concrete areas for improvement.

Develop an action plan: Based on the feedback analysis, develop an action plan that outlines the steps you will take to address the identified areas for improvement. Set clear goals, define measurable objectives, and establish a timeline for implementation. Ensure that the action plan is aligned with your overall execution strategy.

Communicate and involve stakeholders: Share the feedback analysis and action plan with relevant stakeholders, including team members, leaders, and other key individuals. Seek their input and involvement in the improvement process. This collaborative approach fosters a sense of ownership and accountability among all stakeholders.

Monitor progress and adjust: Continuously monitor the progress of your improvement efforts and regularly assess the impact of the changes you have implemented. Adjust your execution plan as needed based on the results and feedback received. Embrace a mindset of continuous learning and improvement.

Leveraging feedback for future execution is a critical component of mastering strategic execution. By actively seeking and embracing feedback, you can gain valuable insights, uncover blind spots, and drive continuous improvement. Remember that feedback is a powerful tool that can guide your decision-making and help you achieve greater success in executing your strategic objectives. Embrace feedback as a catalyst for growth and use it to propel your execution efforts forward.

11. YOUR PERSONAL EXECUTION PLAN

11.1 ASSESSING YOUR EXECUTION SKILLS

In order to master strategic execution, it is essential to assess your current execution skills. This self-assessment will help you identify your strengths and weaknesses, allowing you to develop a targeted plan for improvement. By understanding your execution skills, you can enhance your ability to effectively implement strategies and achieve your goals.

Understanding Execution Skills

Execution skills encompass a range of abilities and competencies that are crucial for successful implementation. These skills include project management, resource allocation, adaptability, leadership, and problem-solving. Assessing your execution skills will provide you with insights into areas where you excel and areas that require further development.

Self-Assessment Process
To assess your execution skills, consider the following steps:

Step 1: *Identify Key Execution Skills*
Begin by identifying the key execution skills that are relevant to your role and the goals you aim to achieve. These skills may include project management, communication, decision-making, teamwork, and adaptability. Make a list of these skills to serve as a reference throughout the assessment process.

Step 2: *Evaluate Your Proficiency*
For each execution skill, evaluate your proficiency on a scale of 1 to 5, with 1 being low proficiency and 5 being high proficiency. Be honest with yourself and consider specific examples or experiences that demonstrate your level of proficiency in each skill. This evaluation will provide you with a baseline understanding of your current skillset.

Step 3: *Identify Strengths and Weaknesses*
Review your evaluations and identify the

execution skills in which you excel (strengths) and those that require improvement (weaknesses). Consider the impact of these skills on your ability to execute strategies effectively. Understanding your strengths will allow you to leverage them in your execution plan, while identifying weaknesses will help you prioritize areas for development.

Step 4: *Seek Feedback*
To gain a more comprehensive understanding of your execution skills, seek feedback from colleagues, supervisors, or mentors who have observed your execution abilities. Their insights can provide valuable perspectives and help you identify blind spots or areas for improvement that you may have overlooked.

Step 5: *Set Goals for Improvement*
Based on your self-assessment and feedback, set specific goals for improving your execution skills. These goals should be measurable, achievable, relevant, and time-bound (SMART goals). For example, if you identified project management as a weakness, your goal could be to complete a project management certification course within the next six months.

Step 6: *Develop an Action Plan*
Once you have set your goals, develop an action plan outlining the steps you will take to improve your execution skills. Break down each goal into

smaller, manageable tasks and establish a timeline for completion. Consider seeking additional training, attending workshops or seminars, or seeking mentorship to support your development.

Step 7: *Monitor and Adjust*
Regularly monitor your progress towards your goals and make adjustments as necessary. Reflect on your experiences and learn from both successes and failures. Continuously seek opportunities to apply and refine your execution skills in real-world scenarios.

Assessing your execution skills is a critical step in mastering strategic execution. By understanding your strengths and weaknesses, you can develop a targeted plan for improvement and enhance your ability to effectively implement strategies. Remember that execution skills can be developed and refined over time with dedication and practice. Embrace the assessment process as an opportunity for growth and commit to continuous improvement in your execution abilities.

11.2 SETTING PERSONAL EXECUTION GOALS
In order to effectively execute strategies and achieve your desired outcomes, it is crucial to set personal execution goals. These goals will serve as a roadmap for your actions and guide you

towards successful implementation. Setting personal execution goals allows you to align your efforts with the overall strategic objectives and ensures that you are focused on the right priorities. In this section, we will explore the importance of setting personal execution goals and provide a step-by-step guide to help you define and refine your goals.

Why Setting Personal Execution Goals Matters

Setting personal execution goals is essential for several reasons. Firstly, it provides clarity and direction. When you have clear goals in mind, you can make informed decisions about where to allocate your time, energy, and resources. It helps you prioritize tasks and activities that are directly aligned with your strategic objectives, enabling you to work more efficiently and effectively.

Secondly, setting personal execution goals helps you stay motivated and committed. When you have a clear vision of what you want to achieve, it becomes easier to stay focused and overcome obstacles along the way. Goals provide a sense of purpose and drive, giving you the determination to push through challenges and persevere until you reach your desired outcomes.

Lastly, setting personal execution goals allows for

measurement and accountability. By defining specific and measurable goals, you can track your progress and evaluate your performance. This enables you to identify areas for improvement and make necessary adjustments to ensure that you are on track to achieve your goals. Additionally, sharing your goals with others can create a sense of accountability, as they can provide support and hold you responsible for your actions.

Step-by-Step Guide to Setting Personal Execution Goals

Reflect on your strategic objectives: Start by revisiting the strategic objectives you have set for yourself or your organization. Consider the broader goals you are working towards and how your personal execution goals can contribute to their achievement. This reflection will help you align your personal goals with the overall strategic direction.

Identify areas of focus: Break down your strategic objectives into specific areas of focus. These can be related to different aspects of your work, such as project management, resource allocation, or leadership development. By identifying these areas, you can ensure that your personal execution goals cover all the necessary aspects of your role.

Make your goals SMART: Ensure that your personal execution goals are SMART - Specific, Measurable, Achievable, Relevant, and Time-bound. Specific goals are clear and well-defined, while measurable goals can be quantified to track progress. Achievable goals are realistic and within your reach, while relevant goals align with your strategic objectives. Lastly, time-bound goals have a specific deadline or timeframe for completion.

Break down your goals into actionable steps: Once you have defined your personal execution goals, break them down into smaller, actionable steps. This will make them more manageable and help you create a roadmap for execution. Each step should be clear, specific, and contribute to the overall achievement of your goals.

Prioritize your goals: Evaluate the importance and urgency of each goal and prioritize them accordingly. Consider the impact each goal will have on your overall strategic objectives and allocate your time and resources accordingly. Prioritizing your goals will help you stay focused and ensure that you are working on the most critical tasks first.

Create a timeline: Establish a timeline for each goal and its associated steps. This will provide structure and help you stay on track. Set deadlines for each milestone and regularly review your progress against the timeline. Adjust the timeline if necessary to accommodate any changes or unforeseen circumstances.

Monitor and evaluate your progress: Regularly monitor your progress towards your personal execution goals. Track your achievements, identify any obstacles or challenges, and make adjustments as needed. Regular evaluation will help you stay accountable and ensure that you are making progress towards your desired outcomes.

Seek feedback and support: Share your personal execution goals with trusted colleagues, mentors, or coaches. Seek their feedback and support throughout the execution process. Their insights and guidance can provide valuable perspectives and help you overcome any obstacles you may encounter.

Remember, setting personal execution goals is an ongoing process. As you progress and achieve your goals, new opportunities and challenges may arise, requiring you to adjust and refine your goals. Stay flexible and adaptable, and be open to revisiting and updating your goals as needed.

By setting personal execution goals, you will be better equipped to navigate the complexities of strategic execution. Your goals will provide clarity, motivation, and accountability, enabling you to effectively implement strategies and achieve your desired outcomes. Embrace the process of goal setting and use it as a tool to drive your personal and professional success.

11.3 DEVELOPING AN ACTION PLAN

Developing an action plan is a crucial step in executing any strategy effectively. It serves as a roadmap that outlines the specific tasks, timelines, and resources required to achieve your strategic objectives. Without a well-defined action plan, your execution efforts may lack direction and focus, leading to inefficiencies and potential failure. In this section, we will explore the key elements of developing an action plan and provide practical guidance on how to create one that drives successful execution.

Setting Clear Objectives

Before diving into the details of your action plan, it is essential to revisit and refine your strategic objectives. Clear and well-defined objectives provide a sense of purpose and direction for your execution efforts. They serve as the foundation upon which your action plan is built.

When setting objectives, it is crucial to ensure they are specific, measurable, achievable, relevant, and time-bound (SMART). Specific objectives clearly articulate what you want to achieve, while measurable objectives allow you to track progress and evaluate success. Objectives should also be achievable, considering the available resources and constraints. They must be relevant to your overall strategy and aligned with your organization's mission and values. Lastly, objectives should have a defined timeline to create a sense of urgency and accountability.

Breaking Down Objectives into Tasks

Once you have established clear objectives, the next step is to break them down into smaller, actionable tasks. Breaking down objectives into tasks helps to create a clear and manageable roadmap for execution. Each task should be specific, with a defined scope and deliverable.

When breaking down objectives into tasks, consider the logical sequence and dependencies between tasks. Identify any critical path tasks that must be completed before others can begin. This will help you prioritize tasks and allocate resources effectively. Additionally, consider the estimated time required for each task and assign responsible individuals or teams to ensure accountability.

Defining Timelines and Milestones

Timelines and milestones are essential components of an action plan as they provide a sense of structure and help track progress. Timelines outline the start and end dates for each task, while milestones mark significant achievements or checkpoints along the way.

When defining timelines, consider the estimated duration for each task and any dependencies between tasks. Be realistic in your estimations to avoid overloading resources or setting unrealistic expectations. It is also important to build in some flexibility to account for unexpected delays or changes in priorities.

Milestones serve as markers of progress and allow you to celebrate achievements and evaluate the effectiveness of your execution efforts. They can be tied to specific deliverables or key events in the project. Regularly reviewing and updating milestones will help you stay on track and make necessary adjustments to your action plan.

Allocating Resources

Resource allocation is a critical aspect of developing an action plan. It involves identifying and assigning the necessary resources, such as personnel, budget, equipment, and technology, to execute the tasks outlined in your plan.

When allocating resources, consider the availability and expertise of your team members. Assign tasks to individuals or teams based on their skills and strengths to maximize efficiency and productivity. Ensure that you have the necessary budget and funding to support the execution of your plan. If resource constraints exist, prioritize tasks based on their impact on achieving your objectives.

Establishing Accountability and Communication

Accountability and communication are vital for successful execution. Clearly define roles and responsibilities for each task and ensure that individuals understand their obligations. Establish mechanisms for regular progress updates and feedback to keep everyone informed and engaged.

Regular communication and collaboration among team members are essential to address any challenges or roadblocks that may arise during execution. Foster an environment of open communication, where team members feel comfortable sharing their ideas, concerns, and suggestions. Encourage collaboration and teamwork to leverage the collective knowledge and expertise of your execution team.

Monitoring and Adjusting the Action Plan

Developing an action plan is not a one-time activity. It requires continuous monitoring and adjustment to ensure its effectiveness. Regularly track progress against the defined timelines and milestones. Evaluate the performance of your execution team and identify any areas that require improvement or additional support.

If deviations or delays occur, take proactive measures to address them. Identify the root causes of the issues and adjust your action plan accordingly. This may involve reallocating resources, revising timelines, or reassigning tasks. Regularly review and update your action plan to reflect any changes in priorities, resources, or external factors that may impact execution.

Developing an action plan is a critical step in mastering strategic execution. It provides a roadmap that guides your execution efforts and ensures alignment with your strategic objectives. By setting clear objectives, breaking them down into actionable tasks, defining timelines and milestones, allocating resources, establishing accountability and communication, and continuously monitoring and adjusting your plan, you can increase the likelihood of successful execution. Remember, an action plan is not set in stone but should be flexible and adaptable to changing circumstances.

11.4 MONITORING AND ADJUSTING YOUR EXECUTION

Monitoring and adjusting your execution is a

critical aspect of mastering strategic execution. It involves continuously tracking the progress of your execution plan, identifying any deviations or obstacles, and making necessary adjustments to ensure that you stay on track towards achieving your strategic objectives. In this section, we will explore the importance of monitoring and adjusting your execution and provide practical strategies to help you effectively manage this process.

The Importance of Monitoring Your Execution

Monitoring your execution allows you to stay informed about the progress of your strategic initiatives and identify any potential issues or risks that may arise. It provides you with valuable insights into the effectiveness of your execution plan and helps you make informed decisions about necessary adjustments or interventions.

By monitoring your execution, you can:

Track Progress: Monitoring allows you to measure the progress of your execution plan against predefined milestones and targets. It helps you identify whether you are on track or falling behind schedule, enabling you to take corrective actions promptly.

Identify Deviations: Monitoring helps you identify any deviations from the original plan. It allows you to spot potential bottlenecks, resource constraints, or other obstacles that may hinder the successful execution of your strategy.

Manage Risks: Monitoring enables you to proactively identify and manage risks associated with your execution plan. By regularly assessing potential risks, you can develop contingency plans and mitigate any negative impacts on your strategic objectives.

Ensure Accountability: Monitoring provides a mechanism to hold individuals and teams accountable for their roles and responsibilities in executing the strategy. It allows you to identify areas where additional support or resources may be required and address any performance issues promptly.

Strategies for Monitoring Your Execution

To effectively monitor your execution, consider implementing the following strategies:

Establish Key Performance Indicators (KPIs): Define specific KPIs that align with your strategic objectives and reflect the critical success factors of your execution plan. These KPIs should be measurable, relevant, and time-bound, allowing you to track progress and evaluate performance accurately.

Implement Regular Reporting Mechanisms: Set up a reporting system that provides timely and accurate information on the progress of your execution plan. This can include regular status updates, performance dashboards, or project management tools that allow you to monitor key metrics and milestones.

Conduct Periodic Reviews and Assessments: Schedule regular reviews and assessments of your execution plan to evaluate its effectiveness and identify any areas for improvement. These reviews can be conducted at predetermined intervals or triggered by significant milestones or events.

Engage Stakeholders: Involve key stakeholders in the monitoring process to ensure their buy-in and support. Regularly communicate progress updates, share insights, and seek feedback from stakeholders to foster a collaborative and transparent approach to execution.

Adjusting Your Execution

Adjusting your execution involves making necessary changes to your plan based on the insights gained from monitoring. It allows you to adapt to changing circumstances, address emerging challenges, and optimize your chances of success. Here are some strategies to help you effectively adjust your execution:

Identify Root Causes: When deviations or obstacles are identified, take the time to understand the underlying causes. This will help you address the root issues rather than merely treating the symptoms.

Evaluate Alternatives: Consider alternative approaches or solutions to overcome challenges or improve performance. Brainstorm with your execution team, seek input from stakeholders, and explore innovative ideas that can enhance your execution plan.

Reallocate Resources: If resource constraints or bottlenecks are identified, consider reallocating resources to ensure optimal utilization. This may involve redistributing tasks, adjusting timelines, or acquiring additional resources to address any gaps.

Communicate and Align: When making adjustments to your execution plan, ensure clear communication and alignment with all relevant stakeholders. Clearly articulate the reasons for the adjustments, the expected outcomes, and any changes in roles or responsibilities.

Monitor and Evaluate: Continuously monitor the impact of your adjustments and evaluate their effectiveness. This will help you determine whether further refinements or interventions are required to ensure the successful execution of your strategy.

Remember, monitoring and adjusting your execution is an ongoing process. It requires a proactive and agile mindset to respond to changing circumstances and optimize your chances of success. By implementing effective monitoring strategies and making necessary adjustments, you can stay on track towards achieving your strategic objectives and master the art of strategic execution.

CONCLUSION

In conclusion, "Your Sixth Move: Mastering Strategic Execution" has been an exploration of the vital intersection between strategy and execution. We've traversed a path that goes beyond traditional business strategies, venturing into the realms of practical execution and results-driven action.

Throughout this journey, you've learned that strategy alone, no matter how brilliant, is only the beginning. The heart of success lies in execution. A well-crafted plan, without effective execution, is like a ship without a captain. You've gained insights into every facet of strategic execution, from the role of project management to optimizing resource allocation and maintaining agility in execution.

By delving into case studies of strategic execution, you've seen firsthand how companies have transformed their strategies into real-world achievements. The ability to overcome common execution challenges is now part of your toolkit, as is the knowledge of the crucial leadership qualities required for effective execution.

Measuring success and embracing a culture of continuous improvement are no longer just buzzwords; they're integral parts of your strategic execution strategy. As you've discovered, metrics and Key Performance Indicators (KPIs) are your compass to assess progress, while the lessons learned from your execution experiences are your stepping stones to continuous improvement.

In the final chapter, you've had the opportunity to create your own personal execution plan. This plan is your unique guide, designed to transform your strategy into action. It's the culmination of your learning and your bridge between where you are now and where you want to be.

So, what's your next move? With the knowledge, strategies, and tools you've acquired in this book, you're better equipped to tackle the complexities of strategic execution. Remember that mastering strategic execution is an ongoing journey, and every day offers an opportunity to apply what you've learned. It's not just a skill; it's a mindset, a commitment to turning plans into reality.

As we wrap up this book, I encourage you to approach your strategic execution with the same passion and vigor that you bring to your strategic planning. The business world is filled with visionary thinkers, but those who can master the art of execution are the ones who turn visions into triumphs. I hope this book has armed you with the insights and inspiration needed to be one of those exceptional few.

Thank you for joining me on this journey of mastering strategic execution. Your sixth move begins now, and it's time to make it count.

ACKNOWLEDGMENTS

Writing a book is not a solitary endeavor, and "Your Sixth Move: Mastering Strategic Execution" is no exception. Many people have contributed their knowledge, support, and encouragement to make this project a reality.

I would like to express my deep gratitude to Patrick Bet-David, whose groundbreaking work in "Your Next Five Moves" inspired the concepts discussed in this book. Your insights have been a guiding light on the path to strategic execution.

I am grateful to OnePurp's team involved in the creation and publication of this book. Your expertise and dedication have been instrumental in bringing these ideas to life.

Last but not least, I extend my appreciation to the readers. Your interest in mastering strategic execution is what drives authors to explore and share these concepts. I hope this book empowers you on your own strategic journeys.

Thank you all for being a part of this endeavor.

OnePurp's CEO